STREETS OF
SAN FRANCISCO

STOCKTON STREET TUNNEL

Streets
of San Francisco

THE ORIGINS OF STREET AND PLACE NAMES

Louis K. Loewenstein

Illustrated by Penny deMoss

Lexikos • San Francisco

ACKNOWLEDGMENTS

While I am completely responsible for this book's contents, I would like to thank the following people whose suggestions and insights only and immeasurably improved it:

Hamilton Barrett; Louis Bernstein; Bob Berlo; Don Burkholder, San Francisco Redevelopment Authority; Josephine Cole; Randolph Delehanty, writer; Sarah Elias, editor; Gladys Hansen, City Archivist and curator of the San Francisco Public Library's History Room; Corbet Hanchett; George Holly, Gray Line Sight Seeing Tours; Robin Kirk, Lexicos Publishing Co.; Karl Kortum, Director of the San Francisco Maritime Museum; Sandra Larson, Librarian of the Presidio Army Museum; Michael Lampen, Archivist, Grace Episcopal Cathedral; Eugene Mattingly, St. Francis Square; James McCarthy, former Planning Director, City of San Francisco; John B. McGloin, University of San Francisco; Frances Roberts, Real Estate Department, Presidio of San Francisco; Edward Roper; Eric Saul, Curator of the Presidio Army Museum; Father Tom Seagrave, Associate Pastor, St. Peter's Catholic Church; Brian Shea; Dr. Charles Albert Shumate, former President of the California Historical Society; Wes Willoughby, San Francisco Redevelopment Agency; and Warren White, City College of San Francisco.

I made extensive use of the following libraries to which I also owe a debt of gratitude: The Bancroft Library of the University of California, the California Historical Society Library, the San Francisco Public Library History Room, and the Sons of California Pioneers Library.

First published in April, 1984 by Lexikos
San Francisco, California

Edited by Robin Kirk. Designed by QR Inc. Produced by Carlton Herrick/QR Inc. Text in Century Oldstyle by Mercury Typography. Printed and bound by Edwards Brothers.

Library of Congress Cataloging in Publication Data

Loewenstein, Louis K.
   Streets of San Francisco
   Bibliography:p
   1. San Francisco (Calif.)—Streets 2. Street-names
—California—San Francisco. 3. Names, Geographical—
California—San Francisco. I. Title.
F869.S375L64 1984 979.4'61 82-49331
ISBN 0-938530-27-5

     86 87 5 4 3 2

CONTENTS

TO
MY
MOTHER
AND
FATHER

In an article about San Francisco streets, the *San Jose Pioneer* of September 15, 1897, noted: "But outside of a few prominent streets ... and those bearing the names of presidents little seems to be known among San Franciscans as to whom and what the pioneers were whose names remain on the maps of their city."

What was true eighty years ago is equally true today. Of course, some books, articles, and newspaper stories on the origins of San Francisco street names have appeared in the past eight decades. But no general work—until this one—has dealt comprehensively with the topic.

For a variety of confounding reasons, any work such as this must be somewhat tentative and incomplete; there are undoubtedly mistakes of both omission and commission in the following pages. For example, despite my best efforts, I was able to discover the origins of the names of approximately 1,200 of San Francisco's 1,735 non-numbered and non-lettered streets. Where I am not positive about the derivation of the name, I have used the words "probably" or "possibly." In some other instances, however, even where this *caveat* is missing, there may still be errors. Naturally, I would like to be made aware of these misstatements so that an improved second edition might appear some day. So I encourage you to submit corrections and additional information to Lexikos, the publisher of this book.

The fact that I was not able to unearth all of the origins of the street names merits an explanation. In the first place, the great fire following the 1906 earthquake destroyed many city records (along with the city's new City Hall). For example, 28 alleys and courts and more than three dozen streets were given new names in 1882. Yet no records explaining who or what these streets were named for exist (see Appendix). The most prolific spate of street naming occurred in 1909 when the Street Names Committee of the Board of Supervisors gave almost 100 streets new names. But for the most part this committee's deliberations appear lost to history. Indeed, the documentation of street names in general is less than one would hope for. Street name changes are approved by the Board of Supervisors after review and approval by the Department of Public Works. But the rationale for these changes does not usually appear in the *Proceedings of the Board of Supervisors* or in the ordinances of the *Municipal Records.* Only the name change itself is to be found. Thus, the researcher is often left to intuition, judgment, and even wits in the search for the origins of street names.

Several guidelines used in the preparation of this book should be mentioned. First, very little anecdotal material is given about well-known figures such as Christopher Columbus. Considerably more biographical data is offered for such local luminaries as James Lick or James Fair. Second, I have tried to find the origin of geographical names, such as Nottingham Place, even though these words are usually taken for granted. Finally, I excluded the names of several street groupings whose origins are obvious. These include streets which were named by the Redevelopment Authority for precious and semi-precious gems in the 1960s, and those of thoroughfares named for trees.

Though San Francisco's streets are constantly being named and re-named, one can distinguish four periods during which the activity was at its height. The first of these is associated with four early surveys of the city which took place in the decade after 1839 when San Francisco was in its infancy.

Before the Gold Rush, the naming of the city streets accompanied the efforts of the municipal surveyors to lay out and map the lots and blocks of the village of Yerba Buena (which became San Francisco on January 30, 1847). In the spring of 1839, Governor Juan Alvarado directed Yerba Buena's *alcalde* (or mayor) Don Francisco Guerrero to have such a survey made of the muddy little community. In the fall of that year, Guerrero chose Jean Jacques Vioget, a Swiss sailor, tavernkeeper, and surveyor, to map the area bounded by Pacific, Montgomery, Sacramento, and Grant Streets. To Grant goes the honor of being San Francisco's oldest street. It was laid out in the late 1830s by William Richardson, the village's first inhabitant, and was called Calle de Fundación, or Foundation Street—an appropriate name for the first street of what was to become one of the world's great cities. Incidentally, Richardson's home, called a "rough shanty of boards" by Richard Henry Dana, was in what is now the 800 block of Grant between Washington and Clay.

In 1846, Lt. Washington A. Bartlett, Yerba Buena's military *alcalde*, commissioned Jasper O'Farrell to resurvey and extend the town. O'Farrell, an Irish engineer who had lived in Philadelphia and Valparaiso, Chile, before coming to California, based his plan on that of Philadelphia, considered at the time an excellent example of urban planning (Vioget was influenced by New York as well). As a consequence some of the street names in these early surveys, such as Broadway and Greenwich were in-spired by New York while others such as Lombard, Sansome, Chestnut, Filbert, Pine, and Market, are borrowed from Philadelphia.

During the Gold Rush, the town exploded in size and O'Farrell fever-ishly continued his surveying by extending the street lines in all directions (including straight into the Bay, thus creating underwater "paper blocks"). O'Farrell also laid out a second gridiron south of the original one which was tilted 45 degrees from the first plan. Between the two grids, O'Farrell planned Market Street, to run from the Bay toward Mission Dolores. The surveys were totally insensitive to the contours of the town's hills and the undulations of its shoreline. They superimposed a dull grid plan—perhaps appropriate for Philadelphia's level ground—onto the won-derfully varied texture of San Francisco's landscape. Thus regularity and consistency dominated and froze into place what could have been an ex-citing and handsome array of streets that respected and enhanced the natural environment. Nowhere is this lack of imagination more evident than in the creation of two separate grids on either side of Market Street. Instead of uniting the city, Market separates it into two distinct areas by creating a traffic pattern that is inconsistent, irregular, and frustrating.

O'Farrell's design was further extended by City Surveyor William M. Eddy in 1849. The urban historian Rodger Lotchin has written, "Given the fact that William Eddy . . . stayed drunk a goodly portion of his working day, it is a wonder that the (plan) turned out as well as it did." The fourth surveyor in this early period was J. J. Hoff about whom very little is known. What is known, however, is that in those days streets tended to be named for pioneers and their friends or relatives, for prominent civic officials or their friends, for the ships which brought settlers to California's golden shores, or for home towns and districts in the East, in England, or on the Continent.

The second street naming phase took place around the Civil War. Patriotic names or names associated with American history became popular. For instance, streets in Noe Valley are named for Civil War battles at Chattanooga and Vicksburg. Real estate developers also began thematic projects. The University Homestead Association, for example, chose the names of prestigious eastern colleges and universities for their streets. A group of streets were named for European capital cities and countries in the 1860s by the Excelsior Homestead Association in what is known today as the Excelsior neighborhood. During this era, as the city expanded in all directions (including into the Bay, where those "paper lots" became landfill), the city fathers used numbered streets and avenues; by 1876, two sets of numbered streets as well as one set of numbered avenues had emerged. This extended Eddy's original numbering system, which had been limited to only five streets.

The third street naming epoch was begun by the 1909 Committee on Street Names. Its charge was to bring a sense of order to what had by now become a chaotic process. The Committee's report acknowledged that "among the conspicuous mistakes are the use of the alphabet and the overworking of the numerals . . . the use of the letters of the alphabet is a cheap and indefensible expedient resorted to only when imagination is lacking." The conscientious street namers observed, "Other California cities of Spanish origin have availed themselves of the musical names associated with its discoverers and founders and made the most of our common inheritance [but] we have made very little of it." So they advocated giving the numbered avenues names which would commemorate saints and men prominent in the days of Spanish rule. The supervisors representing the affected districts objected to the proposal on the grounds that "Spain was one of the most cruel and bloodthirsty nations in Europe . . . and because of . . . the difficulty the conductors on street cars would have in mastering [these names]."

Because of these objections, most of the avenues have retained their numerical designations. But the vast majority of the Committee's recommendations were accepted. About 340 street name changes took effect, though approximately one half were concerned merely with replacing "avenue" with "street" or eliminating "south" from a number of avenues.

The fourth period in street naming took place after World War I and lasted approximately two decades. Here we find private developers—as opposed to public officials—remembering and honoring the city's Spanish heritage. Spanish-sounding street names were selected by realty companies because such names carried an assumed mark of distinction. Such a choice, however, was really nothing new. Throughout its history, San Francisco's developers and contractors have consistently requested that the Board of Supervisors name streets for their friends or relatives, but especially for whatever they considered popular and thus marketable.

In the last few years, however, another strong trend has emerged. Because of the city's changing ethnic composition, many Irish and English street names, names that don't have the same resonance for the newer settlers of Asian or Hispanic heritage are being changed: Lefty O'Doul has become Tandang Sora to remember a Philippine patriot, and South Drive has been changed to Martin Luther King, Jr. Drive to honor the slain civil rights leader. Though some may bemoan the passing of the likes of Lefty (there is still a bridge named after him), they should remember that street names will and should change with the times, with the city they describe and make understandable. And there has never been a city of such glorious and rapid change as San Francisco.

Louis K. Loewenstein
San Francisco
January, 1986

MACONDRAY LANE

CITY STREET NAMES A–Z

ACADIA
Street
Probably named for France's Atlantic seaboard possessions during the 17th and 18th centuries. In turn, Acadia derives from Arcadia, a mountainous district of ancient Greece thought of as the ideal region of rural contentment. North American Acadia included parts of Quebec, Maine, Nova Scotia, and the maritime provinces of Canada. French Canadians deported from Acadia in 1755 for refusing to sign an allegiance to Great Britain migrated to Louisiana; these "Cajuns" flourished in the bayous of the South.

ACEVEDO
Avenue
Luis Joaquin Alvarez de Acevedo was an early settler.

AERIAL
Way
An appropriate name for a street on top of Sunset Heights. At 700 feet, it is the fourth highest peak in the city. Mt. Davidson is the highest at 938 feet, followed by Mt. Sutro (918 feet) and Twin Peaks (903 and 910 feet).

AGNON
Avenue
Brother Agnon was a faculty member of St. Mary's College, then located in a spot to the west of St. Mary's Recreation Center.

AGUA
Way
The Spanish word for "water" is an appropriate name since the street abuts Stanford Heights reservoir.

AHERN
Way
Francis J. Ahern was Chief of Police for two years beginning in 1956.

ALABAMA
Street
Named after the state which was possibly named for an Indian tribe whose name derived from Choctaw *alba*, "thicket" or "plants" and *amo*, "cleaners" or "reaper" or "plant reapers." The territory and state were named for the river.

ALADDIN
Terrace
This thoroughfare was probably named for the Arabic boy, Aladdin, who discovered a genie in an oil lamp. Mark Twain, writing in the *Alta California* in 1866, said of San Francisco, "She is the new Aladdin who shall seize (the lamp) from its obscurity and summon the genie and command him to crown her. . . ."

ALAMEDA
Street
Alameda is the Spanish word for a "tree-shaded poplar grove." The word is derived from *Alamo*, a poplar or cottonwood tree common in Spain. The street was named after the county in the East Bay.

ALBATROSS
Court
The largest seabird, the albatross inhabits only the Pacific and southern oceans.

ALBION
Street
The Roman's name for England, Albion, originally meant "white." When English explorer Sir Francis Drake first came to Northern California in 1579, he called it Nova Albion or New England.

ALDRICH
Alley
Mark Aldrich (1801-1873) has the distinction of being one of three persons whose first and last names are used separately to name two different streets. He is joined by General Winfield Scott and Captain Fernando Rivera y Moncada; the street which claims his given name is Mark Lane. Although Aldrich's life was colorful, no one knows why he was so honored. Born in New York, he moved to Illinois and was elected

to the state legislature in 1836. In 1845, in the town of Nauvoo, Illinois he was tried and acquitted of murdering the visionary founder of the Mormons, Joseph Smith, and Smith's brother Hyrum, as well as of wounding follower John Taylor. Aldrich deserted his family in 1850 and headed for the Gold Rush. Later he turned up in Tucson, Arizona, where he was elected mayor.

ALEMANY **Boulevard** Archbishop Joseph S. Alemany, first archbishop of San Francisco, was born in Spain. After serving as the Bishop of Monterey (1850–1853), Alemany came north where he held his post in San Francisco for thirty-one years. Although he became an American citizen, he eventually returned to Valencia, Spain, where he died in 1888.

ALHAMBRA **Street** Named for the Moorish fortress and palace in the Andulasian region of southern Spain. In Arabic, *alhambra* meant "The Red," referring to the color of the fortress walls. Washington Irving, early American author, based the novel *Alhambra* on this historic spot.

ALLEN **Street** Named for a Scots contractor who sailed around Cape Horn headed for the Gold Rush of 1849. He built the first homes on Leavenworth and Hyde Streets (see also Natick Street).

ALMA **Street** The name is derived from the Spanish word for "soul" and probably honored a pioneer.

ALMADEN **Court** Originally in Arabic and subsequently in Spanish, *almaden* meant "mine." The quicksilver mines of Almaden, Spain, have been in production since Roman times. In the 1800s, the town of New Almaden in Santa Clara County boasted a large quicksilver deposit. Quicksilver, otherwise known as mercury metal, was highly coveted by the Forty-Niners—it was used to refine gold.

ALOHA **Avenue** The all purpose Hawaiian word for "hello", "good-bye" and "love". In the late 1920's Hawaii was a popular tourist mecca and this street which was built in this period was named to take advantage of this allure.

ALPHA **Street** Inspired by the first letter of the Greek alphabet. Alpha is near Delta Street, but neither Beta nor Gamma Street exist.

ALPINE **Terrace** Suggested by the Swiss mountain range, alpine is an appropriate appellation for a street on lofty (510 feet) Corona Heights.

ALTA **Street** The Spanish adjective for "high" is a favorite California place name. Alta Street lies near the top of Telegraph Hill.

ALTA MAR **Way** In Spanish, this means "high sea." Overlooking both the Pacific Ocean and the South Bay, Alta Mar is located in the extreme north west of the city, one block south of Lincoln Park and one block east of Sutro Heights Park.

ALTA VISTA **Terrace** Spanish for "high view," this short street on the slopes of Russian Hill offers an attractive panorama of the City and Bay.

ALVARADO   Juan B. Alvarado was the twelfth governor of Mexican
Street   California, from 1836 to 1842. A central figure in Califor-
nia's history, along with Picos and Castro he led the opposition to the
American occupation. The geographical center of San Francisco (land
only) is on the east side of Grandview Avenue between 23rd and Alvarado
Streets.

ALVISO   Corporal Domingo Alviso and his family of five came with Anza
Street   in 1776.

AMADOR   José María Amador (1794–1883), a native of San Francisco,
Street   was a soldier at the San Francisco Presidio as a young man.
He then became the major domo of Mission San Jose. At 49, he was
granted Rancho San Ramon, a large land tract. Amador is reported to
have shot a hundred Indians after baptizing them.

AMAZON   Ancient Greeks believed a race of female warriors lived on the
Avenue   western fringe of the world. When Francisco de Orellana first
navigated the Brazilian river, he claimed he fought with skillful women
warriors, the Amazons of legend. The river's length is second only to the
Nile's and the area drained is twice as large as the nearest competitor's.

AMHERST   Named after the college named for Lord Jeffrey Amherst, a
Street   British general who fought in the French and Indian war.

ANDERSON   Possibly named for Robert Anderson, a Union General dur-
Street   ing the Civil War. Known as the "Hero of Fort Sumter," he
transferred the northern garrison to this base from Fort Moultrie. Fort
Sumter received the opening bombardment of the Civil War.

ANDOVER   Probably named after the town in Massachusetts which was
Street   named after a town in Hampshire England which was the
home town of several of the original settlers.

ANNA   A popular but unverified story has it that two brothers with the
Lane   name of Lane were to divide a piece of land with the flip of a coin.
The winner was to receive the choice of halves while the loser got the
balance plus the privilege of naming the street along its western boundary.
Hence the name of the loser's daughter, Anna, was chosen.

ANNAPOLIS   After the capital city in Maryland named for Anne Arundel.
Terrace   The Greek word for city is "polis."

ANNE LARSEN   A fitting name for a street in Saint Francis Square, a
Lane   housing project sponsored by the International Longshoremen's Union, located on the Geary Expressway between Webster
and Laguna Streets. The *Anne Larsen* was a three-masted schooner of 376
tons and 48,000 board feet capacity. Built near the turn of the century at
Fort Blakely, Washington, she landed in Federal Court in 1915, mixed up in
the adventures of the little tanker *Maverick*, a gun runner for (rebels) in
India. *The Anne Larsen* ended her wartime activities by being stranded on
Malden Island in 1918 and becoming a total loss.

ANNIE   There are two possible origins for this name. First and most
Street   likely is that it was named by surveyor William Eddy for Jasper

O'Farrell's boat. The other possibility is that it was chosen by early settler Imanuel Charles Christian Russ to honor a daughter.

ANTHONY Street The maiden name of Mrs. William Eddy, whose husband was the city surveyor in 1849.

ANZA Street (Also Boulevard) Captain Juan Bautista de Anza, the "Father of San Francisco," led a sizable party of soldiers and settlers from Sonora, Mexico, to Monterey in 1775 when he was forty. But the journey was slow and Anza was obligated to return to Mexico. Moraga continued on to San Francisco Bay, arriving July 27, 1776. Anza's party located the site for a mission on the shores of what had been named La Laguna de Nuestra Señora de los Dolores and selected a site near the present Fort Point for the Presidio. These 240 soldiers, priests, and settlers preceded the first settlement at Yerba Buena by about sixty years.

ANZA VISTA Avenue "View of or by Anza" in Spanish it is also the name of the neighborhood through which this street runs. Anza's party may have stopped here to view the Bay on their original exploration of this area. The group camped about one half mile away on the evening of March 27, 1776.

APOLLO Street After the Greek god of the sun, constitutions, prophecy, crops, and the arts.

APPAREL Way At one time, this thoroughfare ran through the center of Apparel City, but now all the clothing manufacturers have moved away.

APTOS Avenue For Rancho de Aptos, a Spanish land grant for which the community of Aptos was named. The name is probably the Spanish rendering of a local Castanoan Indian word.

AQUAVISTA Way In Latin, "the view of the water." Almost at the top of Twin Peaks, the Pacific Ocean is just visible over the rooftops.

ARBALLO Drive Señora Feliciana Arballo, widow of a member of the Anza party, brought her two daughters, Tomasa and Estaquio, along on the journey to San Francisco. She later married Juan Franciso Lopez, a mission guard at San Gabriel.

ARCH Street Possibly after the Philadelphia street or an underwater rock in the Bay blown up on August 15, 1901.

ARCO Way Arco means "arch" or "bow" in Spanish.

ARDATH Court Ardath Nichols, a prominent community leader in Hunters Point during the 1960s, was honored with a street in the new development project.

ARELLANO Avenue Manuel Ramirez Arellano, a soldier under Anza, was born in 1742 in Puebla, Mexico. He arrived with Anza's company in 1776.

ARGENT Alley The French word for silver or money.

ARGONAUT Jason and the Argonauts, strong sailors of the ship *Argo*,
   Avenue   desired the fabled Golden Fleece according to Greek
myth. During the expedition, the hardy adventurers struggled against the
elements as well as against men. The early settlers of San Francisco,
nicknamed Argonauts, struggled as well to attain California's fabled gold.

ARGUELLO Commandante José Darío Argüello, Spanish-born Presidio
  Boulevard commander, was the governor of Alta California in 1814.
He is buried in the cemetery at Mission Dolores. His son Luís Antonio,
was California's first native-born governor, the second governor under the
Mexican flag (1822–25), and also a commander of the Presidio.

ARKANSAS For the *Quapaw* tribe of the Sioux. They called themselves
   Street   *Ugakhpah,* "downstream people." The street is named for
the state and the river which were named for this tribe.

ARMISTEAD General Lewis Addison Armistead commanded the Pre-
    Road   sidio in 1859. He was killed in the Battle of Gettysburg
while fighting for the Confederacy.

ARMSTRONG General Samuel Strong Armstrong was the founder of
   Avenue   Hampton Institute, in Hampton-Sydney, Virginia, one of
the first American institutions of higher learning for blacks. Armstrong
was instrumental in helping Booker T. Washington complete his formal
education.

ARMY One of a series of streets in an early Noe Valley subdivision
 Street (c.1860). The developers, John and Robert Horner, purchased a
ranch in this area for $200,000. They laid out the streets, naming some in
honor of branches of military service. They also designated a Navy Street
whose name was subsequently changed to a number.

ARROYO *Arroyo* means "stream" or "creek" in Spanish. It is possible
   Way   that a small stream once ran nearby.

ARTHUR Born in 1831, Chester A. Arthur was the twenty-first presi-
  Avenue   dent of the United States (1881–1884). He assumed the office
after the assassination of President James A. Garfield. His was a moderate administration remembered for a defense budget which included
funds for the first steel-hulled Navy cruisers.

ASHBURY (Also Terrace) Munroe Ashbury served as a member of the
  Street   Board of Supervisors from the fifth ward from 1864 to 1870.
He was instrumental in the creation of Golden Gate Park.

ATALAYA *Atalaya* in Spanish means "watchtower" or "lookout."
Terrace

AVALON In Celtic mythology, Avalon means "the land of the blessed." It
 Avenue   was assumed to be the earthly paradise where enchantress
Morgan le Fay healed King Arthur. Prior to 1907, this street was called
Japan Street.

AVILA After the Spanish province and province capital, Avila, called the
 Street "finest medieval remanent in Spain." It was the home of St.
Theresa. The only son of Ferdinand and Isabella is buried there.

AVON Avon is Celtic for "river" or "water." Several rivers and a river
Way county in England bear the name.

AZTEC After the tribe whose name is probably derived from the Indian
Street word *Aztlán* or "white land." The Aztec believed they were
created in Aztlan, probably northwestern Mexico and southwestern
United States, where they dwelt for over a thousand years. They settled in
the Valley of Mexico now Mexico City. Aztlan was also an early name for
California. The adjacent street, Montezuma, is named for the famed
leader of the Aztecs during the Spanish conquest of Mexico.

BADEN Named after a stop on either the San Francisco-San Jose
Street Railroad or the seashore excursion line which some old
timers called "the peanut special." Near the stop was the Baden
dog racing track. *Baden* is the German word for bath, spa, or hot
springs.

BAKER (Also Court) Colonel Edward Dickinson Baker arrived in San
Street Francisco from Illinois in 1852. One of the City's foremost
lawyers, he was noted for his ability as an orator. Nicknamed "Grey Eagle"
he is credited with bringing California into the Union after a persuasive
speech in what came to be known thereafter as "Union Square." His most
famous defense was of gambler Charles Cora, accused of murdering
Marshal William Richardson in a saloon. Baker argued that the bonds
between prostitute Belle Ryan, whom Richardson had allegedly insulted,
and her lover Cora were as legitimate as any other between man and
woman. He termed it "A tie which angels might not blush to approve." The
jury at the trial was so convinced by his persuasive appeal (and the
admittedly provocative personality of Richardson, a crony of corrupt politi-
cians and gamblers) that they wavered between a verdict of manslaughter
and murder. In the interim, the Vigilance Committee grabbed Cora and
another accused murderer from the jail and hanged them in front of an
angry crowd. A great friend of Abraham Lincoln, Baker was killed in the
Civil War battle of Ball's Bluff. He is buried in the Presidio. The geographical center of San Francisco (land and water combined) is to be found at the
southwest corner of Fulton and Baker Streets.

BALANCE A tiny alley (and perhaps the shortest in the city) named after
Street the sailing ship *Balance* because the ship's timbers were discovered on the site of this downtown street during excavations.

BALBOA Named in honor of Vasco Nuñez de Balboa (1475–1519), who
Street discovered the Pacific Ocean. On September 25, 1513, completing his crossing of the Isthmus of Panama and having climbed a hill
near the Gulf of San Miguel, Balboa saw for the first time what he called
the "South Sea." Impressed by his achievements, King Ferdinand named
Balboa governor of Panama and the Pacific. However, a rival had him
condemned on spurious charges of treason five years later. He was be-
headed in January, 1519.

BALDWIN James Baldwin, novelist, short story writer and playwright
Court wrote *Go Tell It On the Mountain*, *Notes of a Native Son*, and
Nobody Knows My Name. As a spokesman for blacks and civil rights,

Baldwin was honored with a street in predominantly black Hunters Point in the 1960s.

BALTIMORE After the Maryland city which was named for the family of
Way   the Barons Baltimore, the hereditary title of the Calvert
family, who established Maryland in the early 17th century. Cecil Calvert Baltimore founded the only Roman Catholic colony after his father and mother had visited the area during the 1620s and his son succeeded him as proprietor of the colony in 1675. The family's seat was the barony of Baltimore in Ireland.

BANCROFT In 1856, Hubert Howe Bancroft (1832–1918) opened a
Avenue   bookstore in San Francisco, the biggest of its kind west of
Chicago. As a special project, Bancroft started to collect books on California and the West. His collection grew to 60,000 volumes by 1905 at which time he sold them to the University of California for $250,000! He was also renowned for his histories, over forty volumes concerned primarily with the West. He and a host of assistants compiled, wrote, and edited the works between 1869 and 1890.

BANKS Possibly named after Nathaniel P. Banks, a Union general dur-
Street ing the Civil War. Prior to these hostilities, he was a prominent
congressman and governor of Massachusetts; after the war, he returned to Congress. Starting in 1853, he served in ten Congresses, although not continuously. During the war, he fought several engagements against Stonewall Jackson, winning at Kernstown and losing at Cedar Mountain.

BANNEKER Benjamin Banneker, a black surveyor, assisted Major
Terrace   L'Enfant in laying out Washington, D.C.

BANNOCK Probably named after the Great Basin Indian tribe. The
Street   Bannocks were never numerous and probably not more than
2,000 existed at any one time. By 1900, there were only about 500 Bannocks left.

BARCELONA Probably after the Spanish city which was founded by the
Avenue   ancient Phoenicians and Carthaginians and whose name
may be derived from the famous ruling Carthage family, the Barcas.

BARNARD Major General A.C. Barnard was one of the officers in
Avenue   charge of fortifying San Francisco's harbor in 1854. These
installations included batteries at Fort Point, Alcatraz Island, and Lime Rock Point.

BARTLETT Lt. Washington A. Bartlett was the first United States citi-
Street   zen to serve as *alcalde* (chief magistrate) of Yerba Buena
under Spanish rule beginning January 30, 1847. He proclaimed the official name of the city to be San Francisco and designated Washington, Clay, Montgomery, and Sacramento streets.

BARTOL Abraham Bartol, an early settler, was president of the Board of
Street   Assistant Aldermen in 1850.

BATTERY After the city's early fortifications—a battery of cannons
Street   taken from the Presidio in 1847 and erected on Clark's Point
by Lt. Misroon. Situated near the foot of Vallejo Street, it was originally called Fort Montgomery.

BATTERY BLAYNEY Leads to Battery Blayney, in the Presidio,
Road   named to honor Lieutenant Blayney, an artillery
officer and Spanish-American War hero.

BATTERY CAUFIELD Lt. Col. Thomas Caufield died at Letterman
Road   General Hospital on March 6, 1955, after serving forty-four years in the artillery.

BAY Named after the Bay itself which this street once abutted.
Street

BAYSHORE The bay shore once extended to this street.
Boulevard

BAY VIEW Named after the view of the Bay from the western edge of
Street   the street. This is also the name of the neighborhood that
offers a splended view—in places— of the Bay.

BEACH After the beach, which once came up to the street. Because of
Street   land fill, this street is now one block from the beach in the Fisherman's Wharf area of North Beach.

BEALE Edward F. Beale, a naval officer in the Mexican War, brought
Street   camels to California hoping to use them for long haul trans-
portation. The experiment failed. Later, he became Surveyor General of
California and United States Ambassador to Austria.

BEATRICE Beatrice Dunbar was an important community activist in
Lane   the 1960s at Hunters Point.

BEAUMONT "Beautiful Mountain" in French, it is appropriate for a
Avenue   street which runs to and from Lone Mountain.

BELDEN Josiah Belden, born in Connecticut, came to California with
Street   the first overland emigrant party in 1841. A rancher and a merchant he became the first mayor of San Jose. After amassing considerable
wealth, Belden returned east where he died in 1892.

BELLA VISTA At one time, this street, high atop the slopes of Mt.
Way   Davidson, had a beautiful view of the southern portion
of San Francisco and San Bruno Mountain. Now, alas, an array of homes
blocks this view. Bella Vista means "beautiful view" in Italian.

BELLE Probably the first name of someone now lost to history. Although
Avenue this name means "beautiful", this street is anything but beautiful, positioned as it is between two freeways.

BELMONT In French, this means "beautiful mountain."
Avenue

BELVEDERE Italian for "beautiful view," this street lies on an approach
Street   to Twin Peaks.

BEMIS Probably named to honor an individual who fed the homeless after
Street the 1906 earthquake and fire.

BENNINGTON Named after the battle of Bennington in the Revolution-
Street   ary War which took place near the town of the same
name in southwestern Vermont. The town was named after Bennington
Wentworth (1696-1770), colonial governor of New Hampshire (1741-67)

who encouraged settlement in what is now Vermont. He was a founder of Dartmouth College. Another theory is that the name came from Bennington, Hertfordshire, England.

BENTON Named for one of the teachers at St. Mary's College, founded
Avenue in 1863, when it was located in San Francisco.

BERGEN Probably named after the port city in Norway which was that
Alley country's capital in the twelfth and thirteenth centuries.

BERKELEY Bishop George Berkeley was an Irish prelate and philo-
Way sopher (1685–1753). His quotation, "Westward the course of empire takes its way," inspired Frederick Billings to name the East Bay town of Berkeley after him. Berkeley's treatise *De Motu* anticipated Einstein while refuting accepted Newtonian physics.

BERKSHIRE For Berkshire county in England. *Berk* is a British (and
Way Welsh) term meaning "top" or "summit."

BERNAL HEIGHTS Probably named for Don Cornelio de Bernal who
Boulevard acquired the entire territory of what was to become Bernal Rancho from Governor Jimeo Castro in 1839. Don Cornelio's ancestor, Juan Francisco Bernal, was a soldier in Anza's party.

BERNICE Named for a friend or relative of a pioneer.
Street

BERRY Richard N. Berry, born in Massachusetts, was a pioneer mer-
Street chant who emigrated to the Bay Area in 1849.

BERTHA Bertha Freeman was a well-known Hunters Point community
Lane leader in the 1960s when the Redevelopment Authority housing project was in the planning stage.

BERTIE MINOR An appropriate name for a street in a housing project
Lane sponsored by the International Longshoremen's Union. The *Bertie Minor* was a three-masted schooner built in 1864. She carried cargoes of copra and petroleum products. In 1920, while on a voyage from San Francisco to Rabul, New Britain, she had to return to Honolulu for repairs. She was finally laid up in 1924.

BLAKE Prior to 1882, this street was called Ferrie Street. Maurice C.
Street Blake was mayor of San Francisco during that year; the street was probably named for him.

BLANCHE In French, this means "white." The street was probably
Street named for a friend or relative of a pioneer.

BLUXOME Isaac J. Bluxome, Jr., a prominent businessman, com-
Street manded a group of Vigilantes in 1849. He was also secretary of both the 1851 and the 1856 vigilance committees.

BOALT John Henry Boalt, an Ohioan, originally devoted himself to min-
Street ing and mechanical engineering. At the end of the Civil War, Boalt came west to San Francisco. He was appointed to the California Supreme Court and later became its Chief Justice. His widow donated $100,000 to the University of California School of Law, now called Boalt Hall.

BOARDMAN   Possibly named after W.F. Boardman, a prominent sur-
   Place   veyor in the 1860s. Among other projects, he surveyed
Alameda County.

BONIFACIO   Named for a hero of the Philippine struggle against the
   Street   Spanish in the 1890s. The name was changed on August 27,
1979, from Shipley Street since the South of Market area now has a large
concentration of Filipinos.

BONITA   From the Spanish word for "pretty."
Street

BONVIEW   This street was originally called Buena Vista. To avoid confu-
   Street   sion with Buena Vista Terrace and Avenue, the name was
changed. Both names mean "good view" in Spanish and French/English.
The source for this name was the Battle of Buena Vista during the Mexican
American War in which General Winfield Scott became a hero.

BORICA   Don Diego de Borica was governor of California from 1794 to
   Street   1800. This thoroughfare was named in 1909 by the Street Name
Commission which called him "able, honest, and conscientious."

BOSTON SHIP   Named after a merchant ship found in Yerba Buena
   Plaza   Cove, the present site of the Golden Gateway complex
where this plaza is located. Long before the Gold Rush, New England
merchants exchanged Yankee notions with the local residents—
Californios as they were called—for hides and tallow, which were then
shipped around Cape Horn and back to Boston. The leather was made into
shoes, often shipped back to the West Coast for trade.

BOSWORTH   Named by Romain De Boom for a family friend. The De
   Street   Boom family once owned the tract of land where this
street is located.

BOWDOIN   After the college in Maine named for James Bowdoin, a polit-
   Street   ical leader in Massachusetts during the American Revolution (1775–81) and first president of the American Academy of Arts
and Sciences which he founded in 1790. His academic disciplines were
physics and astronomy.

BOWLING GREEN   Named for the lawn bowling game which is played
   Drive   in the outdoor court adjacent to this street in Golden
Gate Park.

BOYLSTON   After the street in Boston probably named for Zabdiel
   Street   Boylston (1679–1766), a Massachusetts physician who
introduced smallpox inoculations to America.

BRADY   Probably named for an early real estate dealer. This portion of
   Street   the city was called "Irish Town" until recent times; it is now
known as "South of Market."

BRANNAN   Samuel Brannan was the leader of the Mormons who sailed
   Street   into Yerba Buena on July 31, 1846. An early jack-of-all-
trades, Brannan started the city's first newspaper, *The California Star*, led
the first vigilante group, announced the discovery of gold at Sutter's Mill,

and sent the first gold nuggets to the Atlantic Coast. Brannan also performed the first marriage and preached the first sermon here under American rule.

BRASIL
Avenue
After the country which was named by the Portuguese for a red plant which was used by the Indians in the northern part of Brasil to color their bodies for ceremonial functions.

BREEN
Place
Patrick Breen was one of the survivors of the Donner party, a group of emigrants who attempted to cross the Sierra Nevada Mountains during the winter of 1847. Breen wrote the record of the ordeal, *Diary of the Donner Party.*

BRET HARTE
Terrace
Easterner Bret Harte—tutor, stage coach messenger, typesetter, newspaper reporter, novelist, and poet— came to San Francisco in 1854 and wrote about the Gold Rush and the pioneers. Perhaps his most famous stories are "Luck of Roaring Camp" and "The Outcasts of Poker Flat."

BRIDGE VIEW
Drive
This street does have a view of the San Francisco— Oakland Bay Bridge as well as a tower of the Golden Gate Bridge.

BRITTON
Street
Joseph Britton was a famous San Francisco based lithographer and a friend of Henry Schwerin who developed the subdivision in which this street is located.

BROAD
Street
Possibly named after the Philadelphia Street which Philadelphians sometimes consider to be the longest straight street in the world. Its twelve mile length, however is exceeded by Chicago's 23½ mile Western Avenue which therefore is the longest straightaway in the United States.

BROADWAY
Named for the famous New York street which acquired its name because of its width. The original name which the Dutch settlers gave to this thoroughfare in what was then New Amsterdam was "Breetweg."

BRODERICK
Street
New York-born David C. Broderick was a San Francisco real estate investor elected state senator in 1850. Under Broderick, the "Tammany Democracy," strongest political organization in the city, flourished. Subsequently, he became a United States senator. He lost his life in a duel with David Terry, recently resigned chief justice of the California Supreme Court, at Lake Merced on September 13, 1859.

BROOKLYN
Place
Probably after the ship which brought Mormon emigrants from the east coast to San Francisco before the Gold Rush. The story goes that the 200 Mormons who landed in 1846 doubled the city's population. In turn, it is likely that the *Brooklyn* was named for an eastern town, now a New York borough, in turn named after a community in Holland.

BROOKS
Street
Named in honor of Col. Horace Brooks, from November, 1872 to January, 1877, Commanding Officer of the Presidio. He died at the age of 84 on January 13, 1894.

BROSNAN Charles W. Brosnan, a native of Ireland, came overland from
Street New York to California in 1850. He practiced law for twelve
years, then moved to Nevada where he became Nevada's first Chief Justice. He died in San Jose in 1867.

BROTHERHOOD A unique highway and private street owned by the
Way religious institutions which line its path. These include
the St. Thomas More Catholic Church, Congregation Beth Israel-Judea,
the Lake Merced Church of Christ, the Holy Trinity Greek Orthodox
Church, St. Gregory, an Armenian church, as well as the Richmond
Masonic Temple and the Brandeis-Hillel Day School. Originally it was
called Stanley Drive, but when these diverse buildings were constructed
the ecumenical spirit prevailed.

BRUSSELS Named for the Belgian capital which is situated on the Senne
Avenue River. At the point where the river and a road crossed a
community arose in the middle ages. The residents called it Bruoc-della
which means the settlement in the marshes.

BRYANT A prominent San Francisco property holder who took an ac-
Street tive interest in politics, Edwin Bryant served as *alcalde* (magistrate) of San Francisco in 1847, succeeding two others who are also honored with streets,Hyde and Bartlett. Bryant favored the sale of beach and
water lots to help raise money for the city treasury. He also invoked the
Mexican law, giving governors of territories the power to make land
grants.

BUCARELI Lt. General Baylio Fray Don Antonio Maria Bucareli y
Drive Ursua, Viceroy of New Spain, sent Colonel Anza north to
establish the Presidio and Mission. He was very interested in the little
community and envisioned a great commercial city on the bay.

BUCHANAN John C. Buchanan, auctioneer and real estate investor, was
Street a prominent local politician. In 1847, he became the chief
magistrate under Mayors Bryant and Hyde.

BUCKINGHAM After the English market town and borough on the
Way River Ouse, site of a Roman settlement and an important pre-Norman conquest stronghold.

BUENA VISTA (Also Terrace) In Spanish "good view." The name,
Avenue however, came from the Battle of Buena Vista during the
Mexican American War in which General Winfield Scott became a hero.

BURKE Edmund Burke was a British statesman and political thinker who
Avenue was prominent from 1765 to about 1795. Important in the history
of political thinking, his policies called for a conciliatory attitude toward the
American colonies and for steps easing the economic and political oppres-
sion of Ireland.

BURNETT Peter H. Burnett was elected the first governor of California
Avenue in 1849. Later, he returned to the practice of law and served
as a justice on the California Supreme Court.

BURNS Probably for a pioneer, several of whom had the last name
Place Burns.

BURR George Burr was General Manager and Chief Engineer of the San
Avenue Francisco Water Department in the early 1960s.

BUSH There are at least four possible origins: 1) after a street in Phila-
Street delphia chosen by Swiss surveyor and sailor, Jean Jacques Vioget,
who laid out San Francisco's streets in 1839, 2) after J.P. Bush, one of
Jasper O'Farrell's assistants. O'Farrell succeeded Vioget as the city engineer, 3) after Doctor J.P. Bush, 4) according to an 1897 issue of the
authoritative *Pioneer Magazine* of San Jose, "Bush Street was not named
for anyone. The late Rear Admiral R.W. Meade, when a small boy was in
San Francisco, and carried the chain for the surveyors, when surveying
the streets. They had given each street a name until they came to this
street when the surveyor asked what shall we call this one, young Meade
pointing to the brush that had caused them so much trouble remarked,
'Why not call it Bush Street?' And Bush Street it was called."

CABRILLO The navigator Juan Rodríquez Cabrillo is considered
Street to be the discoverer of Alta California. He entered San
Diego Bay on September 28, 1542. In the following November, Cabrillo was the first to cruise the Pacific coast from San Francisco as
far as Russian River.

CALEDONIA After the ancient name for an area of North Britain be-
Street yond Roman control, roughly corresponding to modern
Scotland.

CALGARY Probably after the city in Alberta, Canada. Calgary is Gaelic
Street for "clear running water." This town began as a Northwest
Mounted Police post, renamed Fort Calgary in 1876.

CALHOUN John Caldwell Calhoun (1782–1850), a political leader from
Terrace South Carolina, held the offices of United States Congressman, Secretary of War, Secretary of State, United States Senator, and
Vice-President. He was an articulate champion of states' rights and a
symbol of the Old South.

CALIFORNIA According to Michael Venegas, a Mexican Jesuit and au-
Street thor writing in the early 1700s, "This name owed its origin to some accident; possibly to some words spoken by Indians, and mis-
understood by the Spaniards." A more likely possibility is that it first
appeared in the novel *The Adventures of Esplandián* written by García
Ordóñez de Montalvo and published in Toledo, Spain, by 1521. California
was the name given to a fabulous island in the Pacific, rich in minerals and
precious stones and reputed to be the home of a tribe of Amazons, ruled by
Queen Califia.

CAMBON Fray Pedro Benito Cambón, a Franciscan padre with Anza's
Drive party, was assigned to Mission Dolores by Father Junípero
Serra in 1776.

CAMBRIDGE After the University town in England located on the river
Street Cam whose name originally meant a fording place or
bridge.

CAMELLIA A type of evergreen shrub native to East Asia and notable
Avenue for colorful and attractive flowers.

CAMERON Donaldina Cameron, born in New Zealand in 1869, arrived
Way two years later in San Francisco. Her Chinese Presbyterian
Mission was long a haven for Chinese girls who had been sold into prostitution. It was located at the corner of Sacramento and Joice Streets. She
died in 1968 at the age of ninety-nine.

CAMP Named for the first encampment of Anza's party here in 1776. It
Street consisted of a row of tents and shacks about 500 yards east of
Mission Dolores. The soldiers were waiting for a supply ship bringing
provisions to the Presidio.

CAPISTRANO Named for Mission San Juan Capistrano located just
Street north of San Clemente.

CARDENAS Señora Juana Cardenas, wife of Felipe Santago Tapia, accompanied her husband, a soldier with Anza, to northern
California in 1776. She brought nine children with her and had four more
baptized at Santa Clara after 1778.

CARGO A street leading to the piers where ships load and unload cargo.
Way

CARMEL The Carmelite order, whose origin can be traced to Mt. Carmel in Palestine, took its name from the original Hebrew
words "Har Karmel" or "Ha-Karmel." The mountain's name dates back
to biblical times and derives from the Hebrew *kerem,* for "vineyard" or
"orchard." This etymology attests to the mountain's fertility even in
ancient times. In 1602, three friars of the Carmelite order explored Monterey as members of Vizcaíno's expedition.

CAROLINA After the state which was named for Caroline of Ansbach. In
Street 1705 she married a man who became King George II, ruler of
Great Britain from 1727 to 1760.

CARROLL For Charles Carroll, the only Roman Catholic signer of the
Avenue Declaration of Independence.

CARTER Charles D. Carter was a land speculator and real estate broker
Street who published and edited the *San Francisco Real Estate
Circular.* On May 25, 1871 he died of apoplexy at the age of 46.

CASA *Casa* means "house" in Spanish.
Way

CASCADE Probably for the mountain range which extends from Northern California through Oregon and Washington to British
Columbia. The range was named for the great cascades found near the
4000 foot deep Columbia River gorge on the Washington–Oregon border.

CASHMERE Marcalee Cashmere was a prominent community leader in
Court Hunters Point during the mid-sixties when the Redevelopment Authority's project there was in the planning stage.

CASITAS Although there are houses of all sizes along this street, the
Avenue word means "little houses" in Spanish.

CASSANDRA After the Greek mythological figure Apollo fell in love
Court with. He proposed that if she gave herself to him, he
would give her the gift of prophecy.

CASTELO Gertrudis Castelo was the wife of Juan Antonio Vásquez, a
Avenue soldier in Anza's party of 1776.

CASTENADA Named after a member of the Coronado expedition
Avenue (1540–1542).

CASTILLO *Castillo* means "castle" in Spanish.
Street

CASTLE An alley on Telegraph Hill adjacent to Windsor Alley. Windsor
Alley Castle has been one of the principal residences of the British
royal family since the ninth century.

CASTRO Named after General José Castro, a descendent of a member of
Street Anza's original company. At one time, General Castro was in
command of all the Spanish forces in California. Following the occupation
of Monterey and San Francisco by American Forces, he was the most
active opponent to the rule of the United States.

CATHARINE Probably after a friend or relative of an early pioneer.
Court

CAYUGA Named after the Iroquois-speaking Indian tribe which origi-
Avenue nally inhabited central upstate New York by Cayuga Lake.

CEDRO This is Spanish for "cedar."
Avenue

CENTER This street bisects South Park. South Park is one of the few
Place open public areas in South of Market and is located between
Second and Third Streets and Bryant and Brannan Streets.

CENTRAL This street runs through the approximate middle of San
Avenue Francisco. Until 1904, Presidio Avenue was called Central
Avenue.

CERES After the Roman goddess of the growth of grains and food
Street plants.

CERRITOS This word means "little hills" in Spanish, and is an appropri-
Avenue ate name for a street located on one of San Francisco's
numerous little hills.

CERVANTES Miguel de Cervantes was an important Spanish author
Boulevard (1547–1616). Novelist, playwright, and poet, his most
famous work is *Don Quixote*.

CHABOT Anthony Chabot (1814–1888) was a pioneer San Francisco cap-
Terrace italist and philanthropist. One of sixteen children, Chabot was
born in Quebec, Canada and came to California to work in the gold mines
near Nevada City. Called "the father of hydraulic mining," Chabot was the
first to mine gold by moving earth with water pressure. Later Chabot built
San Francisco's first public water system.

CHAIN OF LAKES This road in Golden Gate Park connects a chain of
Drive (East, West)   lakes known as North Lake, Middle Lake, and
South Lake.

CHAPMAN Possibly named for George H. Chapman, a Union general
Street   during the Civil War. During the Pennsylvania campaign,
he led his regiment at Upperville, Gettysburg, Falling Waters, and Brandy
Station. Wounded at a battle in Winchester, Virginia, Chapman recovered
to fight in the Shenandoah campaign.

CHARLTON Perhaps after a dairy or dairy owner. This cul-de-sac is
Court   reputed to have been a milk-wagon loading yard for a dairy
which served the city a century ago and gave this district, Cow Hollow, its
name.

CHARTER OAK Probably after a street of the same name in Hartford,
Avenue   Connecticut, famous for the oak tree which once
shaded it. Legend has it that Captain Joseph Wadsworth hid a Royal
Charter in its trunk. This document gave the residents a claim to a strip of
land as wide as the state itself—fifty miles—and on westward to the
Pacific, cutting a stripe across the continent. The charter was hidden from
Sir Edward Andros, who attempted to seize it in 1767.

CHATTANOOGA After the Civil War Battle of Chattanooga which took
Street   place near Chattanooga, Tennessee, in 1863. The city
derives its name from an Indian expression for nearby Lookout Mountain.

CHESLEY George W. Chesley was a pioneer who arrived in San Fran-
Street   cisco on June 13, 1849, on the steamer *Oregon*. He was in the
auction business for a year before moving to Sacramento to work as a
mercantilist. From 1852 until 1854, however, he returned to San Francisco
and acquired and subdivided the land where this street is located.

CHICAGO Named for the third largest city in the United States. The
Way   derivation of the original Indian word is controversial: skunk,
wild onion, or powerful.

CHILD Originally called the Street of Good Children, the name was
Street   shortened by the 1909 Committee on Street Names.

CHINA BASIN Ships of the Pacific Steamship Company, the *China
Street   Clippers,* tied up near here in the 1860s.

CHRISTMAS TREE POINT This street high atop Twin Peaks during the
Road   1920s was the site of a huge Christmas tree
which the City had erected and lit there.

CHRISTOPHER George Christopher was the Mayor of San Francisco
Drive   for two terms (1956–1964). A bust of him in City Hall
states, "San Francisco was deep in his heart. He served our City with
brilliant efficiency, devoted purpose and tireless devotion."

CHULA Today in Spanish this word means "low-class woman" while in
Lane   early Spanish slang it meant "maiden" or "sensuous girl."

CHUMASERO Maria Angela Chumasero was married to a member of
Drive   Anza's company, arriving at the Bay in 1776.

CHURCH Since Mission Dolores is but one block away this street is its
Street   probable namesake.

CIELITO *Cielito* means "little" or "dear sky" in Spanish.
Street

CIRCULAR As the name suggests, this street curves; however, it does
Avenue   not make a complete circle.

CITYVIEW Off Panorama Drive, this street is located in a subdivision
Way   where all the streets end in "view." A large part of the city
may be seen from this street.

CLAIRVIEW Except for the fact this street is oriented to a different
Court   compass point, the same explanation applies as above.

CLARA After a friend or relative of a pioneer.
Street

CLAREMONT At one time, this street may have had a spectacular, if not
Boulevard   clear, view of the southwest portion of the city; now,
however, the predominant landmark is Mt. Sutro Tower.

CLARENCE Probably named after a friend or relative of a pioneer.
Place

CLARENDON The origin of this street name is uncertain. One opinion is
Avenue   that it was named for first Earl of Clarendon, Edward
Hyde (1609–1674). He was a famous lawyer, the historian of the "Great
Rebellion," and the man who helped put Prince Charles back on the throne
as Charles II. Another equally speculative opinion is that the street was
named for the fourth Earl, George William Frederick Villers (1800–1870),
who served England twice as Foreign Secretary, the last time under Lord
Gladstone. A third version is that the street was named for a New
England-born pioneer named Addison Clarendon.

CLAY Henry Clay (1777–1852), a great orator and patriot, was one of the
Street   most influential political leaders before the Civil War. His ad-
mirers called him "The Great Pacificator" and "The Great Compro-
miser." San Francisco's first cable car ran down a six block stretch of Clay
Street to Kearny Street on August 2, 1873. The street names Clay, Washington, Montgomery, and Kearny have been in use longer than any others.

CLAYTON Charles C. Clayton (1825–1885) was born in England and em-
Street   igrated to America at seventeen. Arriving in San Francisco
in 1848, he became a quicksilver miner, then a gold miner. Returning to the
city, he opened a flour and grain store. He climbed the political ladder,
serving as an *alcalde* (magistrate), assemblyman (1863–64), supervisor
(1864–69), and congressman (1872). In his obituary, a newspaper stated,
"The opinion became quite general that Mr. Clayton was caught trying to
corner the barley market . . . and that his prospective losses produced the
excitement which finally brought about the cerebral apoplexy. His friends
in Oakland state that he was short on barley estimating his losses at about
$25,000."

CLEARY Don Cleary was the City's lobbyist in Sacramento during the
Court   1960s when the Redevelopment Agency designed the Hunters
Point project.

CLEMENT New Yorker Roswell Percival Clement arrived in California
Street   in 1853. An attorney, Clement was a member of the Board of
Supervisors from 1865 to 1867. The idea of extending Golden Gate Park to
the ocean is said to have been his. He was also the lawyer for the San
Francisco Gas Light Company for about 18 years.

CLEMENTINA Probably after a pioneer. The name is derived from
Street   the mythical Roman goddess who personified mercy
and clemency.

CLEVELAND Banker Charles T. Cleveland arrived in San Francisco in
Street   1849.

CLIPPER An appropriate name for a street in this city since the
Street and Terrace Clipper ship was important in the early development of
San Francisco. The necessity of carrying merchandise speedily to a distant market forced New England and New York ship builders and merchants to invent new and superior types of vessels. Hence the clipper was
designed with great length, sharp lines of entrance and clearance and a flat
bottom. The ships cut the time needed to sail from East Coast ports to San
Francisco almost in half.

CLYDE There are two possibilities for the origin of this street name: It
Street   could have been after a pioneer or for the river in Scotland.

COLBY Named after the college in Waterville, Maine, which was named
Street   for local industrialist and textile manufacturer, Gardner Colby.
He gave Waterville College $120,000 and later an additional $80,000 so
the college changed its name to honor their benefactor.

COLE One origin for this name is R. Beverly Cole, M.D., a supervisor in
Street   the 1870s, who was instrumental in the formation of Golden Gate
Park. Dr. Cole was the first president from the West of the American
Medical Association. Another possibility is Cornelius Cole, a New York
lawyer who arrived in San Francisco late in 1849. For a time, Cole mined.
Afterwards, he practiced law in San Francisco and became one of the
principal organizers of the city's Republican party. Cole was elected to the
U.S. House of Representatives in 1863 and to the U.S. Senate in 1866. He
died at the age of 102, the longest living person who ever served as a
Senator.

COLEMAN William Tell Coleman, a prosperous merchant, was head of
Street   the Second Vigilance Committee in 1856. He is remembered
for having defended a merchant, Jansen, in court by encouraging angry
crowds to take the accused, Thomas Berdue, and lynch him by the waterfront. (See Jansen Street.)

COLIN P. KELLY JR. Colin P. Kelly Jr. has the distinction of being the
Street   first American aviator to be killed during World
War II. This occurred on December 7th, 1941. On that day he dropped the
first bomb to sink a Japanese warship near the Philippine Islands. In his
honor, the street's name was changed from Japan Street. The original

name was chosen because of the street's proximity to the old Pacific Mail Steam Ship Company wharf where boats headed for Japan docked.

COLLEGE Avenue and Terrace Before St. Mary's College moved to Oakland and later to its present location in Moraga, this street ran through the heart of the original campus. Now, all that remains of the campus are streets which on a city map have the appearance of a bell. These streets were probably laid out in this fashion to represent the famed Bell(s) of St. Mary's.

COLON Avenue This word is the Spanish form of "Columbus." It is the name of a province and city in Panama, a district in Honduras, and a city in Cuba—all honoring Christopher Columbus who discovered America in 1492.

COLTON Street There are two possible origins. C.O. Colton, a founder of the Southern Pacific Railway or David D. Colton, one of the early associates of Huntington, Crocker, Stanford, and Hopkins, contemptuously known as one-half of the Big Four and One-Half. David Colton was the chief lawyer and financial director of the Central Pacific Railroad. He was also a second to Broderick in his famous duel with David S. Terry.

COLUMBUS Avenue Christopher Columbus, the Italian explorer, discovered America in 1492. Every year on or about October 12th, the discovery is reenacted in the city's Aquatic Park.

COLUSA Place After the tribe of California Indians who once lived along the west bank of the Sacramento River.

COMMER Court Julia Commer was an important community activitist in the 1960s at Hunters Point when the Redevelopment Authority's project there was being planned.

COMMERCIAL Street An early—and at that time, an important—business street which ran from the stores and financial houses down to the wharves and piers along Kearny Street.

COMMONWEALTH Avenue Probably named after the street of the same name in Boston which may have received its name from the fact that Massachusetts (along with Virginia, Pennsylvania, and Kentucky) was a commonwealth rather than a state. In the 17th century, the term was originally used by such writers as John Locke and Thomas Hobbes to mean an organized community.

COMPTON Road Brig. General Charles E. Compton was Commanding Officer of the Presidio on two separate occasions in 1899.

CONCORD Street Probably named for the town in Massachusetts which is the site of the first skirmish of the American Revolution. The area is marked by Daniel Chester French's bronze Minuteman statue. Concord was the first Puritan settlement inland from tidewater and ocean commerce. The name was inspired by the peaceful agreements made with local Indians.

CONGO Street Probably named for the world's second largest river basin (after the Amazon) and the second longest river in Africa (next to the Nile). The name came from the Kongo people who inhabited central Africa; the Kingdom of Kongo was once situated on the lower part of the river's course.

CONNECTICUT Named for the state which was named after the colony
Avenue   and originally the river of the same name. The word means "long river" and comes from the Mohican Indian word *Quonehtacut* or *Quinnehtukguet* or *Connittecock*.

CONVERSE Possibly named for Charles P. Converse, a colorful and
Street   rambunctious character who built the Millerton court house and jail near Friant in the San Joaquin Valley in October of 1867. He had the dubious distinction of being the first occupant of one of the cells since he got into a gun battle shortly after completing construction. Converse had a series of adventures; he married the widow of a county treasurer who mysteriously disappeared—along with a sizable amount of public funds—on a trip with him. Eventually, Converse ran out of money and committed suicide in the bay.

CORA Gambler Charles Cora, who killed United States Marshal William
Street Richardson in a saloon because of an alleged insult to Cora's lover, Belle Ryan, was hanged by an angry mob near the waterfront on May 22, 1856. Cora's lawyer, Colonel Baker (see Baker Street), tried to argue that the ties between Cora and Ryan, a prostitute, were as strong as those of marriage. Responding, a furious resident answered, "Has the man who thus endorsed the sinful union between gambler and prostitute, a mother living?" Cora is buried in the Mission Dolores cemetery next to Belle, who married him on his death bed.

CORAL (Also Court) Probably after the stony skeletons of marine
Road   organisms.

CORBETT After a pioneer family. In the early 1850s, John Corbett was
Avenue   a deputy county clerk. "Gentleman Jim" Corbett, the boxer who fought the great John L. Sullivan is a descendent.

CORDOVA Possibly after the English name for Córdoba, a Spanish city
Street   on the Guadalquivir River. It was the capital of Moslem Spain from the 8th to the 11th centuries.

CORNWALL Probably after the region in the extreme southwest corner
Street   of England settled by Celtic Christians. It was the last part of England to submit to the Saxons and was not completely subjugated until the reign of Edward the Confessor (1042–66).

CORONA After the Spanish name for "crown" derived from Latin for a
Street   "wreath" or "circle." It could also be a last name taken from an early pioneer.

CORONADO Francisco Vásquez de Coronado (1510–1554) was a Spanish
Street   explorer of the North American Southwest whose expeditions resulted in the discovery of the Grand Canyon (1540). He failed, however, to find the treasure-laden cities of Cibola and Quivera he was seeking.

CORTES Hernán Cortés (1485–1547) was a Spanish conquistador who
Avenue   conquered Cuba and Mexico by the time he was 36. He died in
Spain after a disastrous expedition to Honduras.

CORTLAND Probably named for the town in New York State.
Street

COSO The etymology of the word is uncertain. Some believe it to be a
Avenue Shoshone Indian word that means "broken coal" or "burnt
        district."

COSTA The Spanish word for "coast."
Street

COTTAGE Named for the existing cottages on the street acquired and
Row   improved by the Redevelopment Authority.

COUNTRY CLUB A typical subdivision name, Country Club Acres; there
Drive   is no country club nearby, although the zoo and municipal golf course at Harding Park are not far away.

COVENTRY Probably named after the city and district in the West Mid-
Court   lands of England.

CRAGMONT An appropriate name for a street near the top of Sunset
Avenue   Heights—and next to Rockridge Drive.

CRAGS Probably named after the rock formation in adjoining Glen Can-
Court   yon Park.

CRESPI Father Juan Crespí, a Franciscan priest, accompanied Don
Drive   Gaspa de Portolá and Father Junípero Serra on their way north
from San Diego to Monterey Bay. In May, 1770 they founded a mission and
a fort there near the ocean. In 1772, Father Crespí and Lieutenant Fages
journeyed to the Berkeley hills looking for a practical route to Point Reyes
they were thwarted by San Pablo Bay. This expedition pre-dated Anza's
by four years.

CRESTA VISTA In Spanish, this means "view of the crest"—a view of
Drive   Mt. Davidson is obtainable from this street.

CRESTLINE This street approaches the top—or crest—of Twin
Drive   Peaks.

CRESTMONT This name is derived from the location of this street near
Drive   the top of Mt. Sutro.

CRISSY FIELD Named for the currently inactive airstrip in the Presidio
Avenue   which in turn was named to honor Howard Dana Crissy,
a captain in the U.S. Army and a veteran of World War I. Crissy was killed
in his de Haviland aircraft during a transcontinental air race in 1921.

CULEBRA This word means "snake" in Spanish. This little alley is
Terrace   straight, however, and not curved as one might suspect
when thinking about coiled serpents.

CUMBERLAND Named after the river and city in Western Maryland
Street   whose name was taken from an old county in northwestern England. This was also the name of the army during the Civil War –

commanded by Robert Anderson and William Sherman – both of whom have streets in San Francisco named after them. This army covered Tennessee and most of Kentucky at the beginning of the War and later the portion of Alabama and Georgia under Union control.

CUSTER General George A. Custer along with 250 soldiers, was killed
Avenue   in a battle with Sioux Indians led by Chief Sitting Bull, near Montana's Little Big Horn river in 1876.

CYRIL MAGNIN Known as "Mr. San Francisco," this former executive
Street   of the Magnin's retail store is the city's Chief of Protocol.

DAKOTA After the State which was named for the North American
Street   Plains Indians. The name means "allies."

DALEWOOD One of a series of streets in a subdivision known as
Way   "Sherwood Forest." Another street in this area is Robin Hood Drive.

DARIEN Probably after the Isthmus of Darién in Panama, site of the first
Way   attempted European settlement in South America: Santa Maria de la Antiqua del Darién. Here from a hilltop, Balboa first gazed upon the Pacific Ocean. A subdivision called Balboa Terrace is traversed by this street.

DARTMOUTH Named after the college in New Hampshire, which took
Street   its name from the Second Earl of Dartmouth. In turn, his name was taken from the town which lies at the estuary or mouth of the River Dart in Southern England. This is one of a series of streets named for a college or university, by the developers, the University Homestead Association, in the 1860s.

DAVIDSON Professor George Davidson was a surveyor and an expert in
Avenue   land cases. He helped to determine the boundaries between the United States-Canada, and Nevada-California. He became a professor at the University of California; Mount Davidson in San Francisco is named in his honor.

DAVIS William Heath Davis was born in Honolulu and settled in Califor-
Street   nia in 1838. A prominent merchant in San Francisco, Davis also was active as a shipowner and trader. Involved in civic affairs, Davis wrote a book called *Sixty Years in California*, which was recognized as one of the best works on San Francisco's pioneer days. The story goes that Davis raised only white cattle because "he could see them better."

DAWNVIEW A good view of the dawn from this street on Twin Peaks.
Way   Incidentally, the parallel street is Sunview.

DEARBORN Probably named after the city in Michigan which was
Street   named for the Revolutionary War hero, General Henry Dearborn. In 1803, as Secretary of War, he issued an order for a stockade and barracks at "Chicago with a view to the establishment of a Post." This became Fort Dearborn, later Chicago.

DE BOOM Cornelius De Boom was a pioneer and an early Belgian Con-
Street   sul. De Boom became associated with Dr. John Townsend (who also has a street named for him) in the real estate business.

DECATUR Probably named after Stephen Decatur (1779–1820), a U.S.
Street   Naval officer whose ship, the *United States*, captured the
British vessel *Macedonian* during the War of 1812. Decatur is credited with
the expression, "Our country . . . may she always be right, but our country,
right or wrong."

DECKER Peter W. Decker, born in Pennsylvania, arrived at Sutter's
Alley   fort, now Sacramento, via the Overland Route in 1849. Decker
became Mayor of Marysville in 1857 and two years later established a
bank. Although his business interests were elsewhere, Decker purchased
a residence in San Francisco where he lived for a number of years before
his death.

DE HARO Francisco De Haro (1792–1848) was the first *alcalde*, or chief
Street   magistrate, of Mexican Yerba Buena, the little village that
became San Francisco. In 1839, he surveyed the area with the assistance
of Captain Jean Vioget. After his twin sons were murdered by Americans
under Kit Carson's command in 1846, he "declined and died of grief."

DELMAR In Spanish, this means "of the sea." However, it isn't an es-
Street   pecially appropriate name for this street since it is situated
almost in the middle of the city.

DEL MONTE This means "of the mountain" in Spanish.
Street

DEL SUR "Of the south" in Spanish, an appropriate name for this south-
Street   ern street.

DELLBROOK This street originates (or ends) in a group of eucalyptus
Avenue   trees which might be considered a dell and ends (or
begins) across from a dry creek bed.

DELTA After the fourth letter in the Greek alphabet. Alpha
Place and Street Street is nearby, but there is no Beta or Gamma Street.

DE SOTO Ignacio De Soto was a soldier in Anza's expedition to San
Street   Francisco in 1776.

DETROIT After the city and river in Michigan. Situated between Lake
Street   Erie and St. Clair Lake the settlement was founded on July 24,
1701 by a French trader, Antoine de la Mothe Cadillac. He named the fort
Pontchartrain du Détroit after his patron and Louis XIV's Minister of State,
Comte de Pontchartrain. The British later simplified it to Detroit, which in
French means "strait."

DEVONSHIRE Devonshire is a district in Southern England, just east of
Way   Cornwall, home of many American emigrants.

DEWEY Probably named for George Dewey (1837–1917), the U.S. Naval
Boulevard Commander whose men defeated the Spanish fleet at the Battle
of Manila Bay during the Spanish-American War. Dewey was later pro-
moted to Admiral, the highest rank ever granted by Congress. The monument in the middle of Union Square was erected to honor Admiral Dewey.

DIANA Named after the Roman and Greek mythological goddess of do-
Street   mestic animals. With strong associations as a fertility deity, she
was called upon by women to aid in conception and delivery. Her name has

the root di ("to shine") and probably means "Bright One." A number of other streets in this part of San Francisco are also named for mythological gods and goddesses.

DIAZ Possibly named after Manuel Díaz, a Mexican trader and ship-
Avenue master who came to California in 1843. He was serving as an *alcalde* (magistrate) in Monterey at the time of the Mexican occupation. He was also a juryman in the first jury trial held in California (1846). The street could also have been named for Fray Juan Díaz, a Franciscan who accompanied Anza to San Gabriel. Fray Díaz established a mission there.

DIVISADERO Several explanations have been offered. Perhaps, the
Street most reasonable is that this is the Spanish word for "division", a very appropriate name for this street since it was once the dividing line between San Francisco and the Presidio, which in the early 1850's was much larger than it is today. Divisadero represented the western boundary of the city; it was first used to designate the border on a 1856 map of what was (and occasionally still is) known as the Western Addition. Another interpretation is that the word is derived from the Spanish "divisar" which means to gaze from a distance. Lone Mountain was once called El Divisadero. Finally, some suggest that the word is derived from another Spanish word which means summit of a great hill.

DIVISION Named because it separates Potrero Nuevo, an area where
Street the streets run east/west, from the South of Market district, where the streets run a northeasterly/southwesterly direction.

DIXIE This is the popular nickname of the southern states, especially
Alley those that belonged to the Confederacy (1860–65). According to the most common explanation, ten-dollar notes issued before 1860 by the Citizens' Bank of New Orleans, used primarily by French-speaking residents, were imprinted with *Dix* (French for "ten") on the reverse side; hence the land of Dixies meant Louisiana and eventually the whole South.

DOLORES (Also Terrace) These streets were named for the mission and
Street the mission church located alongside. But the official name of the mission is San Francisco de Asís; the nearby body of water once called Laguna de la Nuestra Señora de Los Dolores, Lagoon of Our Lady of Sorrows, gave the Mission its present name. This lake was named after the Virgin of Sorrows because the Spanish explorers discovered it on her feast day.

DOLPHIN After the ocean mammal.
Court

DONAHUE Peter Donahue was called the "father of California Indus-
Street try." He established many enterprises: railroad lines which ran north and south from San Francisco, the Omnibus Street Railroad, the city's first street car line, and the San Francisco Gas Company, the first of its kind in the west. The source of Donahue's wealth, however, was the Union Iron Works which he founded in 1849. This factory turned out stamp mills for the California and Nevada mines, the State's first printing press, the West's first heavy locomotive, and the Navy's first west-coast vessel, *Saginaw*, as well as the warships, *Comanche*, *Oregon*, and *Olympia*.

DONNER George and Jacob Donner led a party of immigrants across a
Avenue   Sierra Nevada pass in 1847. Trapped in early winter snows,
some members resorted to anthropophagy.

DORADO Dorado was one of the developers of the subdivision where
Terrace   this street is located. El Dorado, the legendary city of gold in
the Americas, inspired enough greed in Spanish conquistadors to bring
them over the Atlantic.

DORANTES Dorantes was a member of the Portolá expedition to San
Avenue   Francisco in 1769.

DORCHESTER Probably named after either the English town and coun-
Way   try seat of Dorset, originally called Durnovaria in early
Roman times, or the large village in Oxfordshire, England, whose earlier
names were Dorocina and Dorcic.

DORIC Probably named after the classic Greek column with a channeled
Alley   shaft. The word also refers to a dialect, Doric, spoken by the
Dorians, a linguistically distinct Greek people who conquered the
Peloponnese.

DOW William H. Dow was a leading merchant and shipping master in the
Place   1850s. He was also one of the founders of the Howard Street Presbyterian Church.

DOWNEY Possibly after John G. Downey, Governor of California
Street   (1860–1862). Downey came to California as a Forty-Niner and
worked in the gold mines near Grass Valley.

DOYLE Frank Pierce Doyle was a member of the Golden Gate Bridge
Drive   District from Marin County when the approaches to the Bridge
were built in the 1930s.

DRAKE Probably named for Englishman Sir Francis Drake, circumna-
Street   vigator of the world and the most renowned seaman of the El-
izabethan period. In 1579, Drake anchored just North of San Francisco
and took possession of the surrounding area which he call Nova Albion.
He was alleged to have left behind an inscribed plate; it was discovered in
Marin County in the 1930s, but is now considered to be a hoax.

DRUMM Probably named for Lieutenant Richard Drum, an officer in
Street   the Mexican War of 1848 and later an Adjutant General in the
Pacific. Drum was stationed in San Francisco during the Civil War. There
is only one "m," however, in the spelling of his name—the street may have
been named after John Drumm of Ireland, California, who also served in
the Civil War.

DUBLIN After the Irish capital whose name originated from the fact that
Street   this city lies at the confluence of the River Liffey and the Irish
Sea. The dark bog water made the "black pool" which gave the town its
name – *Dubh Linn* in Irish and *Dyfflin* in the language of the original Norse
settlers. A number of streets in this part of town, the Crocker-Amazon
district, were named for European capital cities.

DUBOCE   Col. Victor D. Duboce headed the first California regiment in
Avenue   the Spanish-American War of 1898.

DUKES   John and Sam Duke were attorneys who gave legal assistance to
Court   the community leaders of Hunters Point during the 1960s when
the Redevelopment Authority's project there was being built.

EAGLE   Possibly named for the sailing ship, *Eagle,* which brought
Street   the first three Chinese persons to San Francisco about
1846. They became servant to a man living at the time on Clay
Street.

EARL   Forty-Niner John O. Earl was a member of the Vigilance Commit-
Street   tee of 1851. Although outside the law, this group of well-meaning
citizens endeavored to impose their idea of order on the city's unruly elements. Later, Earl became a banker.

EASTWOOD   The streets in this Westwood Park subdivision end with
Drive   the suffix "wood." This street is located on the east side of
the tract.

ECKER   Pioneer George O. Ecker was a watchmaker and jeweler. He
Street   became an assistant alderman of San Francisco in 1853.

EDDY   Probably named either for William H. Eddy, who survived the
Street   Donner party of 1847 (although his wife, son, and daughter per-
ished in the Sierra Nevada blizzards) or, as seems more likely, for William
M. Eddy, a city surveyor in 1849. In 1851, Eddy made a new enlarged map
which extended streets laid out earlier by Jasper O'Farrell. In spite of his
drinking, Eddy became the state Surveyor General. Rodger Hotchin has
noted that "given the fact that (Eddy) stayed drunk a goodly portion of his
working day, it is a wonder that the (mapping) turned out as well as it did."

EDGEHILL   Carved on the side of Edge Hill Mountain, the name of this
Way   road was derived from the fact that this street is literally on
the edge of a hill.

EDGEWOOD   The Interior Park Belt is to be found at the southern end of
Avenue   this street. However, the first-time visitor won't see the
woods for the plum trees.

EDINBURGH   After the Scottish capital which was named for the fortifica-
Street   tions on the towering crag which were to become the heart
of the city and which have existed on this rock since at least the sixth
century A.D. "Edin" comes from the Gallic word *Eiden* which may be
derived from *Eden* while "burgh" is the Scottish word for *borough.*

EDITH   Possibly after a pioneer.
Street

EGBERT   Named in honor of Army colonel Egbert, killed in the Philip-
Avenue   pines during the Spanish-American war.

EL CAMINO   Literally, "the road of the sea" in Spanish, an appro-
DEL MAR   priate name for a sea cliff thoroughfare which faces the
Golden Gate.

EL   Named after the county in this state. This word means "the
DORADO gilded one." The Indians of Peru and other South American
countries were constantly directing Spanish explorers to a land of fabulous
wealth reputed to have a king whose body was covered every morning with
gold dust. Thus the phrase "El Dorado" came to mean a region where gold
and other precious metals were abundant.

ELGIN Probably from the Scottish hymn, "The Song of Elgin" based on
  Park   the city in Scotland. The "Park" was added to give more status to
the street by the developers.

ELIZABETH Probably after a pioneer.
  Street

ELLIS Hotel owner Alfred J. Ellis came to California in 1847. He was a
  Street   member of the state Constitutional Convention at Monterey in
1849, a member of The Board of Aldermen, and a sheriff.

ELLSWORTH Possibly named after Elmer Ellsworth, a Civil War hero
  Street   who was famous before this war for organizing the Chicago Zouaves and staging spectacular drill exhibitions throughout the
country. He was killed by the proprietor of the Marshall House Tavern in
Alexandria, Virginia, on May 24, 1861, after removing a Confederate flag
from the roof.

ELMIRA (Also Drive) Probably named after the city in upstate New
  Street   York. In 1828 this city was named for the daughter of an early
settler, Nathan Teall.

EL   The Spanish word for "sunflower."
MIRASOL

EL   *Plazuela* means "small plaza" or "median" in South
PLAZUELA American Spanish.

EL POLIN The name is derived from the spring of the same name in the
  Loop   Presidio. The name is associated with a Spanish legend which
said that all maidens who drank from it during the full moon were assured
to have many children and eternal bliss. Another version of the name's
origin suggests that it was supposedly named by the Miwok Indians who
lived in the area prior to the arrival of the Spaniards. The spring was used
actively by the early soldiers and settlers until 1846.

EL VERANO The Spanish word for "summer." Why this word was se-
  Way   lected, however, remains unknown. What is known is that
no book about San Francisco would be complete without the classic line
attributed to Mark Twain: "The coldest winter I ever spent was a summer
in San Francisco."

EMBARCADERO The Spanish name for "point of embarkation" is an
  (The)   appropriate name for this waterfront street.

ENCANTO The Spanish word for "charm" or, its nearest English equiv-
  Avenue   alent, "enchanting" is an appropriate name for this attractive residential street.

ENCLINE Perhaps named for the fact that this street is situated on a
  Court   slight incline on the slope of Mt. Davidson.

ENTRADA This is Spanish for "entrance."
Court

ERIE Possibly named for the *U.S.S. Erie,* one of the support ships in the
Street bay during the American take-over of San Francisco in 1846. This
ship was named after the Indian tribe of Iroquoian linguistic stock, located
along the southern shore of Lake Erie from western New York to Northern
Ohio. Their name, *erie, erike,* or *eriga* is usually interpreted as "long tail," in
reference to the wildcat or panther. This has resulted in the tribe being
called the Cat Nation.

ESCONDIDO This word means "hidden" in Spanish, an appropriate
Avenue name for this street because it lies secluded near Pine
Lake Park in the southwest portion of the city.

ESMERALDA This word means "emerald" in Spanish.
Avenue

ESPANOLA Espanola Jackson was a prominent community leader in
Street Hunters Point during the Redevelopment Authority's
project there in the 1960s.

ESQUINA *Esquina* means "corner" in Spanish.
Drive

ESSEX Named after the famous warship, the U.S.S. *Essex,* which was
Street commanded by Commodore Porter in the War of 1812.

ESTERO This Spanish word translates as "estuary," but is also used for
Avenue an inlet or lagoon near the sea.

EUCLID Possibly after the street in Cleveland, Ohio, which was named
Avenue for the most prominent ancient Greek mathematician. Euclid
was best known for his treatise on Geometry, *The Elements.* Since surveyors and cartographers made extensive use of his contributions, it is little
wonder that Euclid's name was selected to grace a street.

EUGENIA Popular legend has it that beautiful Eugenia was the daugh-
Avenue ter of the tollkeeper on San Bruno Road before the turn of
the century.

EUREKA This word is Greek for "I have found it," the famous exclama-
Street tion of Archimedes, well-known mathematician and philosopher, after he solved a problem about distinguishing between the mass of
pure gold and gold alloyed with silver by observing the relative dis-
placement of water. The word was adopted in 1850 as California's motto; it
is included in the state seal.

EVANS Rear Admiral Robley D. Evans led vessels from the great white
Avenue fleet of the United States Navy on a world tour in 1907. Dispatched by President Theodore Roosevelt to "show the flag" and display
America's military power, the arrival of these ships in San Francisco harbor produced a large burst of social activities.

EWER Possibly named for Ferdinand Ewer, a pioneer journalist and
Place minister.

EXCELSIOR This word means "more lofty" and "elevated" or "higher"
Avenue   in Greek, and is an appropriate name for a street leading to
the hills of McLaren Park.

EXECUTIVE PARK Named for the office park in which this road is
Boulevard   situated.

EXETER Probably named after the cathedral city situated on the River
Street   Exe in southwestern England.

FAIR James G. Fair was born in Dublin in 1831 and first worked in
Avenue California as a pick and shovel miner. A rival of Comstock
Kings Ralston and Sharon, Fair eventually became a U.S. Senator.
In the city's first act of redevelopment, "Bonanza Jim" assembled
the block on which the Fairmont Hotel is now situated. He intended
to build for his family a grand mansion, but his marriage broke up
before he was able to construct the house.

FAIRFAX Probably named for Charles ("Lord") Fairfax of Fairfax
Avenue   County, Virginia, who settled in Marin County in 1856.

FAIRMOUNT This street once led directly to Fairmount Plaza (now
Street   Fairmount Park) and both the street and the park are located in what was once the Fairmont Tract.

FAITH The street next to it is Joy. Obviously, this street was named for
Street   basic human belief. It is also possible that the name honors a
Protestant pioneer.

FALLON Thomas Fallon, a Canadian, arrived in 1844 to take an active
Place   part in the Bear Flag Revolt two years later. Fallon was the first
to raise the United States flag in San Jose. He went on to become a successful placer miner and San Francisco businessman.

FALMOUTH Probably named after the town in Cornwall, England,
Street   which received its name from its location near the mouth
of the River Fal.

FANNING Charles Fanning was a well known engineer who worked for
Way   the City's Real Estate Department. He was in charge of the
property transactions for the Golden Gate Heights project carried out
in the late 1920's by San Francisco's chief engineer, Michael M.
O'Shaughnessy.

FARALLONES In Spanish this means "headland" or "high rock which
Street   stands out in the sea." Even though the seven islands are
about 32 miles out to sea, they are a part of the city.

FARRAGUT Admiral David Glasgow Farragut fought in the War of 1812
Avenue   at the age of eleven. In the 1840s, Farragut was sent to
California from Washington to establish the Mare Island Navy Yard near
Vallejo.

FARVIEW One of a series of streets in a subdivision, each possessing the
Court   suffix "view." The name rings true since this street is situated on the slopes of Twin Peaks.

FAXON Probably named for Faxon Dean Atherton, a large land owner in
Avenue San Mateo County.

FEDERAL Probably named for the United States bonded warehouse
Street once located nearby.

FELL Merchant William C. Fell, born in Denmark, arrived in San Fran-
Street cisco in 1849. He was a member of the Society of California
pioneers.

FELTON Charles Norton Felton (1832–1914) came to California during
Street the gold rush and went into the pickle business. He made his
fortune, however, by investing in the mines of the Nevada Comstock Lode.
Later, he developed the Snow Mountain Water and Power Company in
Lake and Mendocino Counties. He served as an assemblyman and con-
gressman, and replaced U.S. Senator George Hearst after Hearst's death.

FERNWOOD After the plant. One of a series of streets in Westwood
Drive Highlands which have the same suffix.

FILLMORE Named after Millard Fillmore (1800–1874), the 13th Presi-
Street dent of the United States who served from 1850 to 1854. A
moderate Whig politician, his insistence on federal enforcement of the
Fugitive Slave Act of 1850 alienated the North and led to the demise of the
Whig party.

FITCH George K. Fitch was a well-known pioneer and newspaperman.
Street He was co-owner of the *Alta California*, the *Call*, and *Bulletin*
(which he edited from 1856 to 1897). Under Fitch, the *Bulletin* waged a
war for economy in municipal financing and decried the domination of the
Republican and Democratic parties by the Southern Pacific railroad.

FLINT Named for Addison R. Flint about whom little is known.
Street

FLORIDA Named for the state which in turn was named after the Spanish
Street word for "flowering." The area was named by Ponce de Leon
who discovered it on Easter Sunday *(Pascua Florida)* in 1512.

FLOOD James Clair Flood's home is now the Pacific Union Club on Nob
Avenue Hill's California and Mason Streets. Flood arrived in California
during the gold rush and he, James Fair, John MacKay and William S.
O'Brien became known as the Bonanza Kings; they all made their fortunes
mining silver in Nevada.

FLORA Probably from the Roman mythological goddess of budding
Street springtime, fruit trees, vines, and flowers. It also might have
been the name of a pioneer.

FLORENCE Possibly after the Italian city which was originally called
Street Florentina—"the flourishing town." This street also may
have been named for a pioneer.

FLORENTINE (see above)
Avenue

FOLSOM Captain Joseph L. Folsom came to San Francisco as an officer
Street in Stevenson's regiment of 1847. Folsom made and lost a fortune in real estate. He was notorious for hiring thugs to force squatters off
property. He founded the town bearing his name on the American River
which he carved out of a large land grant acquired from the Liedesdorff

family. He, along with millionaire Sam Brannan, were among a long list of landed men who paid no taxes—the city government was not yet powerful enough in 1855 to face down its barons.

FONT Father Pedro Font was a chaplain with Anza's party on their
Boulevard journey from Mexico to San Francisco in 1776. A diary entry on March 27, 1776, reads "The port of San Francisco is a wonder of nature, and may be called the port of ports, on account of its great capacity and the various heights included in its litoral or shore and in its islands."

FOREST KNOLLS This road bisects the Forest Knolls subdivision
Drive where many streets are named after trees. A knoll is an appropriate designation for this area since it is situated on the slopes of Mt. Sutro.

FOREST SIDE Situated on the side of a nameless hill, an abundance of
Avenue eucalyptus, pine, bottlebrush, and palm trees dot the sidewalk which, although not creating a forest, does produce a sylvan setting. This street also marks the western edge of Sutro Forest and Rancho San Miguel.

FOREST VIEW This road ends (or begins) at Eucalyptus Drive. At the
Drive present time, however, one can find neither these trees nor a forest in the vicinity, although Stern Grove and Pine Lake Park are not far away and may have been the inspiration for these names.

FORTUNA In Italian mythology, Fortuna was the goddess of good for-
Avenue tune -an apt appellation for this short residential street.

FRANCE After the country whose name was derived from the Franks
Avenue which occupied the area in the middle ages.

FRANCISCO Probably named after Saint Francis of Assisi, for whom
Street this city was named. (See the Landmarks section of this book for a more detailed discussion.)

FRANCONIA There once was a road house with this name on the toll
Street road which is now San Bruno Avenue (located nearby). In turn, the roadhouse was named for an area which is now part of Germany. Originally inhabited by the Franks who settled there in the 6th century A.D., it includes Bavaria, Baden-Württemberg, Hessen, East Franconia, and Rhineland-Pfalz.

FRANKLIN This street may have been named for either Selim Franklin,
Street a pioneer merchant, or Benjamin Franklin (1706–1790), the noted printer, author, investor, scientist, and diplomat who helped write both the Declaration of Independence and the United States Constitution.

FREELON T.W. Freelon, an active magistrate and county judge of the
Street Court of Sessions, administered the oath of office to Mayor S.P. Webb in 1854.

FREEMAN Named in honor of Brig. General Henry B. Freeman, com-
Court manding officer of the Presidio for twenty days in April, 1899. He received the Medal of Honor for saving a wounded fellow officer under fire during the Civil War.

FREMONT General John Charles Frémont (the son of a Frenchman –
Street   hence the accent mark) took an active part in the Bear Flag
Revolt and the conquest of California. Frémont was briefly the civil and
military governor of the state, a U.S. Senator from California (1849), and
an unsuccessful candidate for president in 1856. Although a Southerner by
birth, Frémont remained in the Union Army during the Civil War because
he was opposed to the secession.

FRESNO Named after the city, which in turn was named—in Spanish—
Street   for the ash tree, which is to be found in abundance in this area.

FRIENDSHIP This thoroughfare is situated in Friendship Village, part
Court   of the Western Addition A-II Redevelopment Project.
The name was selected for the sponsors of the project: The First Friend-
ship Institute Baptist Church.

FRONT At one time, this street was on the shoreline. After the Bay was
Street   filled in, it receded several blocks behind the waterfront.

FUENTE Pedro Perez de Fuente was an early settler.
Avenue

FULTON Possibly named after either an early pioneer, Daniel J. or the
Street   inventor of the steam boat, Robert.

FUNSTON Named in 1923 in honor of Brigadier General Frederick
Avenue   Funston, acting commander of the Army's Pacific Division
during the difficult days after the 1906 earthquake and fire. Funston's
forces were in charge of maintaining law and order in the devastated
streets. Funston Avenue is situated between 12th and 14th avenues and
would be 13th Avenue if it were not for the evils superstitiously associated
with that number.

GABILAN The Spanish word for "sparrow hawk." There are
Way   several other streets with Spanish names in this part of
the Outer Sunset district.

GALILEE A fitting name for a street in St. Francis Square, a housing
Lane   project sponsored by the International Longshoremen's
Union. The *Galilee* was a two-masted brigantine that sailed the South Seas
carrying lumber and may have set a Tahiti-run record for speed. She
was built at Benicia between 1890 and 1901 by Matthew Turner, a famed
shipbuilder.

GALINDO José Galindo owned 2,220 acres of land within the present
Avenue   city limits of San Francisco.

GALVEZ Don José Gálvez, Visitador-General of Spain and a member of
Avenue   the Council of the Indies in Mexico City, organized, equipped,
and dispatched the expedition commanded by Portolá in 1769.

GARCES Fray Francisco Garcés, a Franciscan padre, accompanied
Drive   Anza to San Gabriel, a mission town several miles east of
present-day Los Angeles. Father Garcés and Captain Rivera y Moncada
(for whom two streets were named) were en route to California with a
group of settlers via the Sonora Trail in northern Mexico when they were

ambushed by the Yuma Indians. The entire party was massacred on July 17, 1781. (See also Moncada Way.)

GARCIA Avenue   Garcia is a common Spanish surname.

GARDEN Street   This block-long alley may have been the site of a garden at one time, but now only a few homes and parking lots are to be found along its edges.

GARDENSIDE Drive   Situated on the side of Twin Peaks, this street may have been the location of a garden in former years, but now, alas, only small apartment buildings are to be found on either side.

GARLINGTON Court   Ethel Garlington was a well-known community leader during the 1960s at Hunters Point when the Redevelopment Authority's project there was being developed.

GARRISON Avenue   Cornelius K. Garrison became San Francisco's fourth mayor on October 1, 1853, only six months after his arrival. Born near West Point, New York, Garrison became a ship builder on the Great Lakes before moving to San Francisco during the Gold Rush. After his mayoral term, he became an insurance agent. Garrison returned to New York in 1859 and became a successful businessman.

GATES Street   Horatio Gates (1728-1806) was a general during the Revolutionary War. His major victory over the British at the Battle of Saratoga in 1777 turned the tide of victory in behalf of the colonists.

GATE VIEW Court   This street affords a view of the Golden Gate, hence the name.

GAVEN Street   Gaven was a surveyor and draftsman employed by the Crocker Banking and Land Company. He helped lay out the Crocker estate where this street is located and probably named it after himself.

GAVIOTA Way   Spanish for "seagull," these birds may be seen from this street on the lower slopes of Mt. Davidson.

GEARY Street   (Also Expressway and Boulevard) John White Geary was San Francisco's last *alcalde* and first mayor (elected under the new city charter in 1850). In recognition of services during the Mexican War, President Polk appointed Geary as San Francisco's first Postmaster. Geary gave the city land now known as Union Square. After leaving the city, Geary became a general in the Union Army during the Civil War. Later, Geary had the unusual distinction of being elected Governor of Kansas and subsequently Governor of Pennsylvania.

GENEBERN Way   Brother Genebern was one of the original faculty members of St. Mary's College, once located where the street is to be found today.

GENESSEE Street   Probably named for the region in upstate New York. The word was originally an Indian one.

GENEVA Named after the city in upstate New York which, in turn, was
Street named after the well-known city and lake in Switzerland. The
original name of Geneva (or Genava) dates back to the pre-Celtic Ligurian
peoples. This is but one of a series of streets named for upstate New York
cities. Niagara and Seneca Avenues, for example, are nearby.

GENOA After the port city in Italy. The original name of Genoa (or
Place Genova) is also derived from the pre-Celtic Ligurian people.

GEORGE George Williams was a prominent community leader in Hunt-
Court ers Point during the 1960s when the Redevelopment Authority's project was being built.

GERKE Henry Gerke arrived in San Francisco in July, 1846, and was an
Alley original member of the Board of Directors of the Society of California Pioneers. Gerke was a successful wholesaler of native wines and
brandies, therefore, he was one of the largest taxpayers in San Francisco,
paying $755 in 1850.

GERMANIA As early as 1855, a community of five to six thousand Ger-
Street mans and their families was located in the section of San
Francisco known as Duboce Park. At the foot of the park, this street was
obviously named after their native country. Franklin Hospital which is
situated in this area, was once called German Hospital.

GIANTS This street situated within sight of Candlestick Park was
Drive named after San Francisco's baseball team. It may well be the
only street in America carrying the name of a National (or for that matter
American) League baseball club.

GIBSON Named in honor of Brig. General Horatio G. Gibson, who was
Road post commander of the Presidio in 1856 and on two different
occasions in 1859. When he died in 1924 at the age of 94, Gibson was the
oldest living graduate of West Point.

GILBERT Lieutenant Edward Gilbert was a member of Stevenson's
Street Regiment in 1847, a group of soldiers from New York who
came to California for adventure and to liberate, if necessary, California
from Mexican control. A printer by trade, Gilbert was editor of the *Alta
California* and later, a California congressman. He was killed in a duel at
the age of 30.

GILMAN Daniel Coit Gilman was an American reformer of higher edu-
Avenue cation. As president of the University of California, Gilman
advocated giving less attention to classical subjects.

GILROY Probably named for John Gilroy, the first permanent, non-
Street Spanish settler in California. In 1814, this Scottish sailor either
deserted or was put ashore at Monterey because of scurvy. His name was
Cameron but, being a minor, he adopted his mother's maiden name for
fear of deportation.

GLADVIEW One of a series of streets with the suffix "view" in a sub-
Way division off Panoramic Drive.

GLENBROOK   "Glen" is a Celtic word meaning "narrow valley." It was
   Avenue   an obsolete geographical name revived by the Romantic
movement in the 19th Century.

GLENVIEW   One of a series of streets with the suffix "view" in a sub-
   Drive   division on the south slope of Twin Peaks. This street affords a view of Glen Park.

GOETHE   Johann Wolfgang von Goethe (1749–1832), a German, is a gi-
   Street   ant of world literature. Critic, journalist, painter, theater manager, statesman, novelist, educator, playwright, poet, scientist and natural
philosopher, Goethe is best-known for his drama, "Faust."

GOETTINGEN   Probably named after the town in West Germany.
   Street

GOLDEN GATE   Originally called Tyler Street for John Tyler, tenth
   Avenue   president of the United States, the street became
Golden Gate Park's driveway in 1880 after the Park's opening. General
John Charles Frémont first coined the expression "Golden Gate." (For
more on this subject see the section on Landmarks in this book).

GOLD MINE   Named for Gold Mine Hill around which this street winds.
   Drive   It was named by the Redevelopment Authority in the
              mid-sixties.

GOLETA   This is the Spanish word for "schooner." There are several
   Avenue   other Spanish names on parallel streets in this subdivision.

GONZALEZ   José Manuel Gonzalez, born in Sonora, Mexico, brought his
   Drive   wife and four children when he came to San Francisco in
1776 with Anza's party.

GORDON   George C. Gordon was an Englishman who in the early 1850s
   Street   developed South Park as a select residential area for wealthy
families. He also helped establish the city's first Immigration Society in
1855. They were committed to making the Bay Area a more attractive
destination for immigrants by lowering fares, encouraging vigilante
groups, and hastening the completion of a transcontinental railroad.

GOUGH   Charles H. Gough, a busy milkman, rode through San Francisco
   Street   on horseback with a milk can on either side of his saddle in the
1850s. By 1855, Gough had been appointed to a committee to name the
streets of the Western Addition – so he named one for hismelf. (See
Octavia Street).

GRACE   Named for a relative or friend of a pioneer.
   Street

GRANADA   Probably named for the city and province in southern Spain.
   Avenue   The name may have been derived from either the Spanish
for "pomegranate," a locally abundant fruit that appears on Granada's
coat of arms, or from its Moorish name, Karnattah (Gharnatah), which
possibly means "hill of strangers."

GRAND VIEW   (Also Terrace) A street that lives up to its name—a
   Avenue   splendid view of the city available along its way. The

geographical center of the city (land only) lies between 23rd and Alvarado Streets on the east side of Grand View Avenue.

GRANT Avenue Ulysses S. Grant was General of the Union Army for part of the Civil War and the eighteenth president of the United States. In 1876, the section of this street from Bush to Market was changed from Du Pont Street to Grant Avenue. In 1908, this name was extended all the way to the Bay. Du Pont Street had been named for Captain Samuel F. Du Pont, a naval officer of the *Conquest* and a friend of Washington Bartlett, for whom a street is also named. Grant Avenue is considered to be the oldest street in the city – it was originally called Calle de la Fundación. The first building in San Francisco, a semi-permanent tent, was erected by William Richardson on June 25, 1835 at what is now 827 Grant Avenue.

GREAT Highway In its day (and for that matter even today), this road, which parallels the Pacific Ocean on the city's western edge, was literally a great highway with two lanes of traffic in each direction, separated by a parking area.

GREEN Street Talbot H. Green was a leading merchant who acquired considerable property and wealth in the ten years prior to 1851. In a letter, Green once wrote: "The traders [here] are a sharp set, dog eat dog." While a candidate for mayor, Green was recognized as Paul Geddes, an embezzler who had left his wife and children in the East. Immediately, Green left for the East, claiming he could disprove the charge. He never did. He was, however, taken back by his wife and family—and repaid the money he owed.

GREENVIEW Court One of a series of streets with the suffix "view" off Panoramic Drive in a subdivision on the northwest slope of Twin Peaks.

GREENWICH Street (Also Terrace) Named by Jean Jacques Vioget after a street with the same name in New York City. Vioget, a Swiss sailor and surveyor, laid out many of San Francisco's streets in 1839. The street in New York was probably named after Greenwich, England, through which the mean time meridian passes. It is also the home of the British Naval Academy. Greenwich was mentioned in a document dated 913 A.D. as Gronwic, the original Anglo-Saxon name.

GREENWOOD Avenue One of a series of streets in a Westwood Park subdivision with the same suffix—"wood."

GRIFFITH Street Millen Griffith, a well-known pioneer, arrived in San Francisco in 1849. Capitalizing on the needs of the harbor, he operated a small carrier business, which soon expanded into a fleet of tug boats. In addition, Griffith was a partner in the Pacific Steam Whaling Company.

GRIJALVA Drive Sgt. Juan Pablo Grijalva was born in 1742 in Sonora, Mexico. A sergeant in Anza's party, Grijalva brought with him his wife and three children.

GROVE Street It is not unreasonable to imagine that this street, parallel to and three blocks from Oak Street, was named after a grove of trees or some other comparable vegetation.

GUERRERO   Don Francisco Guerrero was a highly respected Mexican
   Street   citizen who held local offices before and after the Ameri-
can occupation of 1846. Guerrero owned much of what is now San
Francisco.

HAHN   John Hahn was president of the Visitacion Valley Homestead
   Street   Association as well as a property owner in that neighborhood
in the late 1860s.

HAIGHT   There are three versions of the possible origin of this street
   Street   name. The most likely candidate is Henry Haight, a Supervisor
and a manager of the early banking firm of Page, Bacon, and Company.
Since he gave the land for it, Haight was instrumental in the founding of the
Protestant Orphanage. A less likely namesake is Fletcher M. Haight,
Henry's brother, who was a prominent lawyer and later a United States
district judge. The third and least likely prospect is H. H. Haight, an early
California governor.

HALE   John Hale was a leader in the Irish community of the Outer Mis-
   Street   sion. He was employed by the Crocker Land and Banking Company, at one time the owners of the land where the street is located.

HALLECK   Major General Henry W. Halleck, a lawyer, army officer,
   Street   and expert on fortifications, was appointed Secretary of
State of California in 1847. He is reputed to have drafted parts of the
California Constitution. Halleck also served as commander of the Union
Army from 1862 to 1864. Halleck funded the construction of the Mont-
gomery Block, since destroyed to make way for the Transamerica Build-
ing, the tallest building in San Francisco.

HAMILTON   After the college and town in New York, named for Alex-
   Street   ander Hamilton, the first Secretary of the Treasury and a
champion of a strong central government for the former colonies. Hamilton was the primary author of *The Federalist Papers*; he died after a duel
with Aaron Burr.

HAMPSHIRE   Probably named after New Hampshire which, in turn,
   Street   was named for the district in south central England. Both
this and the adjacent street, York, which is also named for an English
geographical area, were probably the homes of early settlers.

HANCOCK   Possibly named after John Hancock (1737-1793), a leader in
   Street   the American Revolution and as president of the Continental
Congress he was the first person to sign the Declaration of Independence.

HANOVER   Probably named after the district and city (Hannover) in
   Street   western Germany which may have been the birthplace of a
          pioneer.

HARDIE   Named in honor of Major General James A. Hardie, the first
   Street   commanding officer of the Presidio under the United States
          flag.

HARDING   This road leads to Harding Park golf course. Both the park
   Road   and the road were named for Warren G. Harding, twenty-
ninth President of the United States (1921–23). Harding died un-
expectedly in San Francisco's Palace Hotel during his third year in office.
His term is remembered for widespread corruption.

HARE   Named for Elias C. Hare about whom not much else is known.
Street

HARLAN   George W. Harlan, his wife, and four children led an overland
   Place   party to California in 1846. He soon enlisted in the Army and
fought in the Mexican War. After his discharge, the family purchased a
ranch between San Jose and San Francisco; they were the only Americans
between the two communities.

HARNEY   Charles L. Harney was an important builder of the mid-
   Way   twentieth century in San Francisco. Candlestick Park was one
   of his projects.

HARRIET   Named for a daughter of Immanuel Charles Christian Russ,
   Street   who owned the nearby amusement park, Russ Gardens.

HARRIS   Probably named for Stephen R. Harris, mayor of San Fran-
   Place   cisco in 1852. Harris was a physician who came to California in
June, 1849. He was the fourth President of the Society of California Pio-
neers; after his term, Harris served as Controller, then Coroner of the city.

HARRISON   Probably named for Edward H. Harrison a port collector
   Street   and a member of the town council shortly after arriving in
San Francisco in 1847. He subsequently became a prominent merchant. A
less likely namesake is William Henry Harrison, the ninth President of the
United States and the first to die in office (1841). He ran on the slogan of
"Tippecanoe and Tyler too."

HARTFORD   Named after the city in Connecticut named after the English
   Street   town, Hertford. The spelling difference may have been due
to the pronumciation of the English name.

HARVARD   Named after the university which was named for John Har-
   Street   vard, a Puritan minister who left his books and half his estate
to the college in the 1630s.

HAVENSIDE   A haven, perhaps, for the fourteen houses which occupy
   Drive   this street, but other than this explanation, the reasons for
this street's name remains obscure.

HAWES   Horace Hawes was a prominent lawyer during the Gold Rush
   Street   and was chief executive officer of the city under the first Mayor,
John W. Geary. Hawes later served in the State Assembly and Senate
where he introduced a bill consolidating the City and County of San Francisco, the only joint city-county in California. (Denver and Philadelphia
share this same distinction in Colorado and Pennyslvania).

HAWTHORNE   Probably after a ship that brought a pioneer to
   Street   California.

HAYES   Colonel Thomas Hayes was the County Clerk from 1853 to 1856.
   Street   His brother, Michael, was one of three members of the committee which named the streets in the Western Addition, and was probably
responsible for this street name. Hayes was also developer of Hayes Valley and fought in a duel with John Nugent.

HEARST George Hearst was born in 1820 in Franklin County, Missouri.
Avenue A Forty-Niner, he struck it rich in Virginia City, Nevada, with
the Comstock Lode, an especially rich vein of silver. Hearst purchased the
San Francisco *Examiner*, which his son, William Randolph, used as the
flagship of his vast empire of newspapers, radio stations, movie studios,
and publishing houses. George Hearst was appointed a United State Senator and successfully ran for reelection in 1886.

HELENA For the woman's name or for the capital city of Montana which
Street was also named for a woman's forename.

HENRY ADAMS Henry Adams was a realtor who developed Showplace
Street Square and the Galleria, both wholesale trade centers
located on this thoroughfare. This street was formerly part of Kansas
Street, but after Adams died of a heart attack in 1980 this portion of the
street was renamed in his honor.

HERMANN Sigismund Hermann (1816–1890) was born in Mecklen-
Street burg, Germany, and arrived in San Francisco in 1849. One
year later, Hermann opened a dry goods and general merchandise business which lasted two decades. In addition to being a successful merchant,
Hermann was briefly an insurance agent, a member of the Board of Trade,
a real estate investor, and a hops trader.

HERNANDEZ Hernandez is a common Spanish surname.
Avenue

HERON Ensign James H. Heron was born in Richmond, Virginia, in
Street 1827. Heron first arrived in California in 1846 on the U.S.S.
Levant. After fighting in the Mexican War, he returned to California
in 1862. Starting as a messenger, Heron worked for Wells Fargo and
Company for 26 years. His final position with the company was that of
Secretary.

HIDALGO In the early Middle Ages, this was a Spanish term denoting
Terrace hereditary nobles and knights. Later, it became a common
Spanish surname.

HIGH Certainly the highest short—shortest high—street in San
Street Francisco.

HIGUERA Ygnasio Anastasio Higura was born in 1753 in Sinaloa, Mex-
Avenue ico, and came with his 13 year old wife to San Francisco in
1776 with Anza's party. Two years later, their son was baptized at Mission
Dolores.

HILL Appropriately named for a street that goes up and down a steep
Street incline on the eastern slope of Twin Peaks.

HILL POINT This street climbs up (or down) the hill towards the top (or
Avenue bottom) of Mt. Sutro.

HILLCREST An appropriate name for this little street almost atop the
Court city's highest peak—Mt. Davidson.

HILLWAY This street also climbs down (or up) the hill towards the bot-
Avenue tom (or top) of Mt. Sutro.

HINCKLEY William S. Hinckley arrived in San Francisco in 1830. An
Walk *alcalde* in 1844, Hinckley later became captain of the Port
and eventually mayor.

HOFFMAN Named in honor of Brig. General William Hoffman, Com-
Street manding Officer in the Presidio for a brief period in 1859. At
one time during his military career, Hoffman was captured by rebels in
Texas and subsequently exchanged for a rebel prisoner.

HOLLAND Democrat Nathaniel Holland was an assistant alderman in
Court 1851; three years later, he was elected to the State Assembly.

HOLLISTER Sergeant Stanley Hollister of California was killed in Cuba
Avenue during the Spanish-American War.

HOLLOWAY Possibly named after William Holloway who came from
Avenue New York City in 1883. He died from a horseback fall
eleven years later. Holloway's career included being the United States
consul to Peru and Uruguay.

HOLLY PARK Since this street completely circumscribes Holly Park, it
Circle is appropriately named.

HOLLYWOOD This street is situated in a subdivision which was
Court marketed as, and is still known locally as Little Hollywood. It is doubtful, however, if even a starlet ever lived here.

HOLYOKE Named after the college which was named for the explorer,
Street Elizor Holyoke. This is one of a series of such streets in this
part of the city that are named for colleges or universities.

HOMER Probably named after the Greek poet and author of the *Iliad* and
Street *Odyssey*, the two greatest poems of Ancient Greece. Almost
nothing is known of Homer's life although scholars believe he was an
Ionian who lived in either the ninth or eighth century B.C.

HOMEWOOD (Also Terrace) One of a series of streets in Westwood
Court Highlands which have the same suffix.

HOOKER Probably named after Joseph Hooker, a Union General during
Alley the Civil War. Prior to his service in the military, Hooker was a
farmer. While a colonel in the California forces, he had a major disagree-
ment with General Halleck for whom a street, several blocks away, is also
named. The expression "hooker" is said to have been derived from the
girls who followed General Hooker's army around the countryside. As
commander of the Army of the Potomac, he successfully defended Baltimore and Washington, although he lost to General Robert E. Lee at
Chancellorsville.

HOPKINS Probably named in honor of Mark Hopkins (1813–1878). Hop-
Avenue kins came to California in 1849 and became a partner of Collis
P. Huntington in a general merchandise store in Sacramento. This led
Hopkins into the "Big Four" as one of the builders of the Central Pacific
Railroad where his principal duties were to supervise and control the fi-
nances of the railroad and its many affiliated companies.

HORACE Street Named after the outstanding Latin lyric poet and satirist whose patron was the emperor Augustus (65 B.C.-8 B.C.). Horace's most frequent themes are love, friendship, philosophy, and the art of poetry. This street is but one block away from a street named for another Roman poet, Virgil.

HOTALING Place Anson Parsons Hotaling was born in New Baltimore, New York. While still a young man, Hotaling sailed around Cape Horn, arriving in California in 1852. After working briefly in the placer mines, Hotaling made his fortune operating a wholesale liquor business. He also owned real estate in San Francisco, Marin, and San Mateo counties and founded a savings bank in San Rafael.

HOUSTON Street Named after the city in Texas, which was named for Samuel B. Houston, the first President of the Republic of Texas (1836–38; 1841–44). In 1836, two New York land speculators bought a site near the burned-out village of Harrisburg, Texas; two months later, one of them proposed that the first Congress of the Republic of Texas, then in session at Columbia, move the government to his town. After much persuasion, Congress agreed. The government, however, stayed only two years before the maneuver was denounced as corrupt. After Texas joined the Union in 1845, Samuel Houston became a senator.

HOWARD Street William Davis Merry Howard was one of the town's most public-spirited and prosperous men. A merchant, Howard was known as the first citizen of San Francisco in the period just before the gold rush. In 1847, he was elected to San Francisco's first City Council—four years later, Howard was one of fourteen persons who organized the first Vigilantes. Later, Howard organized the city's first fire company.

HUDSON Avenue Henry Hudson, the English navigator, discovered the Hudson River and Hudson's Bay while trying to find a shorter route from Europe to Asia.

HUGO Street Victor Hugo (1802–1885), the French poet, dramatist, and novelist, was the most important of the French romantic writers. In later life, Hugo used his great power to shape French public opinion. He is best-known for his novel *The Hunchback of Notre Dame*. A street one block away is named for another author, Washington Irving.

HUMBOLDT Street After the County and Bay of the same name, named in honor of the famed German naturalist, Baron Alexander von Humboldt.

HUNT Street Henry Brown Hunt (1836–1893) was a pioneer merchant. A native of New Jersey and New York, Hunt arrived in San Francisco in 1849. Hunt held a variety of jobs in the gold country and in Sacramento until he formed a wholesale liquor firm in San Francisco in 1880.

HUNTERS POINT Boulevard (Also Expressway) This street is named for the area through which it goes. In turn, the area received its name from one of two possible sources. In 1849, Robert E. Hunter and his brother, Philip Schuyler, participated in the foundation of a new city which was to be called South San Francisco. Alternatively, this area was long called Hunters Point because city sportsmen went hunting there.

HUNTINGTON Collis P. Huntington came west by way of Panama with
Drive   the Forty-Niners. Trading with miners, he became a
merchant and operated a store in Sacramento. Huntington was one of the
"Big Four" along with Crocker, Stanford, and Mark Hopkins; they built
the Central Pacific, the first transcontinental railroad.

HURON Named for the Iroquois-speaking North American Indians who
Avenue   lived along the St. Lawrence River when it was discovered by
the French explorer Jacques Cartier in 1534.

HYDE George Hyde arrived in California in 1846. About a year later,
Street   Hyde was appointed *alcalde* (magistrate) of San Francisco following Bartlett and Bryant (for whom streets were also named). Hyde had
been Commodore Stockton's secretary.

ICEHOUSE Formerly Gaines Street, this thoroughfare was named
Alley   after the two ice houses situated on either side of it—
they are now occupied as offices.

IGNACIO A common spanish surname.
Avenue

ILLINOIS After the state which was named for the Indian tribe of the
Street   same name. These Indians called themselves the *Inini,*
"perfect and accomplished men." The French called them *Illini* and added
the suffix *-ois* to denote the tribe. In the mid seventeenth century there
were some 6,500 such Indians living in what is now southern Wisconsin,
northern Illinois and parts of Iowa and Missouri, but by 1800 only 150 of
them remained alive.

INCA The *Inca,* built in 1896, was a five-masted schooner, the second of
Lane   her rig on the Pacific Coast. On October 10, 1920, she left Eureka
bound for Sydney with a cargo of redwood lumber. On December 7th, she
was dismasted and abandoned by all but two of her crew. Eleven days
later, she was found and towed into Sydney harbor where she was sold for
scrap. With a rich history like this, it would seem only appropriate that a
street in her honor be named in a housing project sponsored by the International Longshoremen's Union.

INDIANA Named after the state which was named for the latinized form
Street   of *Indian* meaning "land of the Indians." Originally the word
referred to the territory which was carved out of the Northwest Territory
in 1800.

INDUSTRIAL As the name implies, industry—or at least distribution,
Street   wholesaling, and automotive repairs—is to be found on
this street.

INFANTRY Named in 1923 after this branch of the Army—an appropri-
Terrace   ate name for a street in the Presidio.

INGALLS Named for General Rufus Ingalls who among other things
Street   was an early land owner in Benecia.

INGERSON Named for Doctor H.H. Ingerson, an early citizen of San
Avenue   Francisco.

INNES Named for George Innes (1825–1894), the noted American
Avenue painter, known for the luminous quality of his later landscapes.

INVERNESS Named for the town in west Marin County which was
Drive probably named for the county and town of the same name
in Scotland.

IRIS Named after either the flower or the Greek mythological female
Avenue figure who was the personification of the rainbow as well as the
messenger of the gods.

IRONSHIP Named after ships often found in Yerba Buena Cove, the
Plaza present site of the Golden Gateway complex where this
street is located. During the closing decades of the last century, American
grain was the principal cargo of deepwater vessels sailing around cape
Horn to Europe. The American ships, called Down-Easters, were built of
wood, but England had exhausted its forests in the Napoleonic Wars and
in about 1850 started to build their sailing ships out of iron. As many as 550
sailing ships were required to haul a single season's grain harvest; two-
thirds of them were British iron vessels.

IRVING Named for Washington Irving (1783–1859), the author who was
Street called, among other things, "first American man of letters,"
"dean," or "father of American literature." Irving's greatest literary success was *The Sketch Book*. This street is located near Hugo Street, while
Goethe and Shakespeare lie much further south.

ISIS Named after the *Isis*, a clipper ship which brought pioneers to San
Street Francisco. The name is taken from one of the more important goddesses of ancient Egypt. Her name is the Greek form of the ancient Egyp-
tian hieroglyph meaning "throne."

ITALY Named after the country whose name comes from the Itali peo-
Avenue ple – a primitive indigenous population who once lived in the
eastern Italian region known as Lucania.

JACKSON Named for Andrew Jackson (1767–1845), the seventh
Street president of the United States and military hero of the
War of 1812. He was the first president from west of the Appa-
lachians to be elected and the first to gain office by a direct appeal to
the voters. His political movement has since been known as "Jack-
sonian Democracy."

JAMESTOWN Probably named for the first permanent British set-
Avenue tlement in North America, founded on May 14, 1607, in
Virginia. This community was named in honor of King James I of England. Jamestown, Rhode Island, was named in honor of King James II,
and Jamestown, New York, was named after James Pendergast, who in
1811 selected the site for his mill, the nucleus of this community. These
other towns may also have been the source for the name of this avenue.

JANSEN Possibly named for a pioneer merchant whose greatest claim to
Street fame is that he was beaten and robbed in late February, 1851.
This and similar crimes produced in turn and time the Committee of Vig-
ilance which established patrols against fire, theft, and other misdeeds.
(See Coleman Street).

JASON According to Greek mythology, Jason was the leader of the Argo-
  Court   nauts, sailors on the ship *Argo*. Early San Franciscans were
called Argonauts because of the hazardous journey they braved to reach
California in search of gold. Jason was promised his inheritance if he acquired the fabled Golden Fleece, a seemingly impossible task. After many
adventures, however, he was able to get it. (See Argonaut Avenue.)

JAVA Probably named after the fourth largest island in the republic of
Street   Indonesia. East of Sumatra and west of Bali, this island was an
important one to early San Francisco—all the West Coast's coffee was
shipped from Java until a crop failure forced Americans to turn to Costa
Rica for their brew in the 1850s.

JEFFERSON (Also Square) Probably named for Thomas Jefferson
  Street   (1743–1826), third president of the United States, principal
author of the Declaration of Independence, first Secretary of State,
founder of the University of Virginia, and an influential political leader
and philosopher.

JENNINGS Named for Thomas Jennings, Sr., a San Francisco pioneer
  Street   who was active in civic affairs. His son, Thomas Jr., was a
member of the Board of Supervisors in 1900–01 and again in 1908–09.

JERSEY Probably after the islands in the English channel governed by
Street   Great Britain.

JESSIE Selected by Immanuel Charles Christian Russ to honor a mem-
 Street   ber of his family. He developed Russ Gardens, an amusement
park, which was located nearby.

JOAQUIN A common Spanish surname.
  Street

JOHN Named after the disciple "whom Jesus loved" and who may well
Street   have been the author of the fourth book of the New Testament, the
Gospel of Saint John, as well as the three Epistles of John and the Revela-
tion. On another note it is ironic that Hooker Street is nearby.

JOICE There are two possible explanations for the origin of the name.
Street   One source is John Joice, a land owner, about whom little is known
other than he sold a lot to James Lick in 1848. The other is Erastus V. Joice
whose home once stood at 807 Stockton. At one time he owned the
Knickerbocker House Hotel and was reputed to have hunted in the area
where this narrow street is located along Nob Hill. Joice Street was once a
service alley and stable entrance when elegant residences graced Stockton
Street.

JONES Named after either Dr. Elbert P. Jones who was the first editor of
Street   the *California Star,* San Francisco's first newspaper. In addition
to owning the second hotel building in San Francisco, he was elected to the
first town council under American jurisdiction in 1847 and he took an active
part in political affairs. Or named after Commodore Thomas A. Jones who
planted the first American flag on California soil when he captured
Monterey in 1842.

JOOST In 1891 Behrend Joost built the electric streetcars which con-
Avenue   nected Glen Park to the rest of San Francisco.

JORDAN James Clark Jordan (1850–1910) owned the Jordan tract,
Avenue formerly the site of an old race track and now called Jordan
Park. Born in Boston, Jordan graduated from Harvard and entered the
family's real estate business. He moved to San Francisco in the 1890s
primarily for his health. Jordan allowed American soldiers to camp on his
land prior to their departure for the Philippines during the Spanish-
American War.

JOSEPHA Señora Josepha Petronila was the wife of a member of Anza's
Avenue party which came to San Francisco in 1776.

JOY The street next to this one is Faith; obviously, these streets were
Street named after basic human emotion and belief.

JUAN BAUTISTA Probably named for either Juan Bautista de Anza (for
Circle a more complete biographical description, see his
entry under Anza Street) or for Saint John the Baptist.

JUDAH Theodore D. Judah was born in Connecticut and arrived in San
Street Francisco in 1854 at the age of 28. A civil engineer, Judah constructed a railroad from Sacramento to Folsom and designed a transcontinental railroad line over the Sierra Nevada Mountains. He was out-
manuevered by the Big Four and consequently lost his share of his
partnership in the Central Pacific Railroad to them.

JUNIPER Probably named after the *Juniper*, a clipper ship which
Street brought pioneers to California.

JUNIPERO SERRA Fray Junípero Serra established the first mission in
Boulevard California in 1769. For many years, Serra served as
the very energetic and capable father-president of all the missions.

JUSTIN Named for Brother Justin, a leader of the Christian Brothers
Drive when they came to take over St. Mary's College, once located
near this street.

KANSAS After the state which was named from the Sioux
Street language: *Kansa* meaning "people of the south wind."

KATE Named after a friend or relative of a pioneer.
Street

KEARNY General Stephen Watts Kearny, in command of an expedition
Street sent to conquer and occupy New Mexico and California, came
west in 1846. A year later he was appointed military and civil governor of
California. He granted the water lots to the town of San Francisco. On this
street, the world's first cable car made its first public trip on June 28, 1873.
Along with Montgomery, Washington, and Clay—the names of other
streets—Kearny has been in continuous usage as a street name longer
than any other. In 1854 the portion of Kearny Street between Washington
and Clay Streets was paved making it the city's first such street.

JOHN F. KENNEDY This thoroughfare in Golden Gate Park was origi-
Drive nally called North Drive, but was renamed to honor
the thirty-fifth president of the United States. Kennedy was the first
Roman Catholic to become president and he launched the Peace Corps and
Alliance for Progress as well as programs in outer space. He was assas-
sinated on November 22, 1963.

KENSINGTON Probably named after Kensington, England.
Way

KENWOOD One of a series of streets in Westwood Highlands which
Way have the same suffix.

KEY Francis Scott Key was a lawyer and author of the United States
Avenue national anthem, the "Star-Spangled Banner." He died in 1843 at
the age of 64.

KEYES (Also Alley) Brig. General Erasmus D. Keyes was the command-
Avenue ing officer of the Presidio for six years starting in November,
1849 and again from October, 1856 to June, 1858.

KEZAR Mary A. Kezar gave $100,000 to the city in 1923 to erect a
Drive stadium which was subsequently named after her. Completed in
1926, it is located in Golden Gate Park.

KING Probably named for T. Butler King, who arrived on the *Panama* in
Street 1847. He was an agent for the United States to California before it
became a part of the union; or possibly named in honor of James King of
William, a crusading newspaper editor, who was shot by James P. Casey, a
supervisor, in the street. Casey had been angered by a muckraking series
in King's newspaper which exposed corruption. Casey, along with gambler Charles Cora (see Cora Street) were hanged by an angry mob on the
day King was buried.

KINGSTON Possibly named after the city in New York State or the bor-
Street ough in Pennsylvania. Both of these communities as well as
others with the same name were named after Kingston-upon-Thames, a
royal borough in London. In turn, this name was derived from the Saxon
word *Cyningestun*, or "king's town."

KIRKHAM Named for Brigadier General Ralph W. Kirkham who
Street fought in the Mexican War of 1847 and the Civil War. He was
in the quartermaster corps.

KIRKWOOD Named for Samuel J. Kirkwood, a wartime governor of
Avenue Iowa.

KISSLING Kissling once owned property where the street which bears
Street his name is located.

KNOLLVIEW One of a series of streets whose suffix is "view" in a re-
Way sidential subdivision off Panoramic Drive.

KOBBE Named in honor of Major General William A. Kobbe. At one
Avenue time, Kobbe was an artillery officer at the Presidio.

KOHALA Named after the volcanic mountain range situated on the
Road northern part of Hawaii.

KRAMER Jacob Kramer operated a grocery store in the vicinity of this
Place street in 1856. After he died, his family continued the business until the fire of 1906.

KRONQUIST Named after the developer of this area about which not
Court much else is known.

LA   In Spanish this word means "a grove of soldiers which
AVANZADZ   advances to observe the enemy at close range" and
this may not be the worst name to describe this street proceeding as
it does up Mt. Sutro to the television tower.

LA BICA   *Bica* is a kind of cornbread eaten in Mexico.
Way

LA GRANDE The name of this street belies the fact that it is only one
Avenue   block long.

LA   Spanish for "beach," this is an appropriate name considering
PLAYA   that the beach probably ran up to this street at one time. Sand
dunes still do abut this thoroughfare.

LA SALLE   Robert Cavalier, Sieur de la Salle (1643–1687) was a French
Avenue   explorer who discovered the Ohio river. La Salle established
France's claim to Louisiana and the Mississippi Valley.

LAFAYETTE General Marquis de Lafayette was an American Rev-
Street   olutionary hero (1757–1834). Born into a noble French
family, Lafayette aspired to glory as a soldier. He came to America to help
the colonists in the Revolution. Lafayette became friends with General
George Washington, and persuaded Louis XIV to send a 6,000–man expe-
ditionary army to aid the rebels.

LAGUNA   This is Spanish for "lake." At one time, a small lake known as
Street   Washerwoman's Lagoon existed one-half mile southwest of
Fort Mason. In early times, most of the laundry for the town was done
there.

LAGUNA HONDA This street runs by a reservoir at the edge of Sutro
Boulevard   Forest where there was once a deep lake. In Spanish,
this means "deep lake." Actually, the street was named after the Laguna
Honda Home which was named for the lake.

LAGUNITAS This word in Spanish means "little lakes," but the street
Drive   was named after the small town in western Marin County.

LAKE   After Mountain Lake, which abuts this street.
Street

LAKE FOREST Situated in Forest Knolls, a subdivision on the slopes of
Court   Mt. Sutro where all the streets have sylvan names, this
street reminds one neither of the famed Chicago suburb nor of a body of
water.

LAKE MERCED This lake was named by the Spanish *Laguna de
Boulevard   Nuestra Señora de la Merced*, the Lake of our Lady
             of Mercy.

LAKE MERCED HILLS Named after Lake Merced.
North/South

LAKESHORE (Also Plaza) This street derives its name from the fact
Drive   that it follows the configuration of Lake Merced.

LAKEVIEW This street has no view of a lake now, but perhaps might
　　Avenue　　 have once when Lake Geneva, now gone, was at the corner
of Niagara and Delano Streets.

LAKEWOOD Although neither a lake nor a wood is evident from this
　　Avenue　　 street, a large number of bottlebrush trees provide a sylvan setting for this thoroughfare, situated in Mt. Davidson Manor where
many streets have this suffix.

LANE Doctor L.C. Lane, a prominent physician, founded Cooper Medi-
Street cal School, once Stanford Medical School, and now the Pacific
Medical Center.

LAPHAM Rodger D. Lapham (1883–1966) served as the thirty-second
　　Way　　 mayor of San Francisco from 1944 to 1948. When elected he
said, "four years will be long enough." A graduate of Harvard, he worked
for and eventually became president of the family-organized and owned
American Hawaiian Steamship Company. This street is adjacent to a
street named for the thirty-third mayor, Elmer Robinson.

LAPU LAPU Named for the Filipino whose army repulsed the invasion of
　　Street　　 Ferdinand Magellan, the Spanish explorer, who was killed
when he and his conquistadors landed in the Philippines in 1521. The street
name was changed in 1979 from Maloney Street to Lapu Lapu in recognition of the growing Filipino community South of Market. Peter Maloney
once was one of the most important businessmen in this area.

LARKIN Multi-talented Thomas O. Larkin arrived in California in 1831
　　Street　　 and had a store in Monterey for many years. Larkin was the
first and only consul to the Mexican government; he was also a secret
agent for the United States, trying to arrange an American occupation of
California without war. A local correspondent for several New York newspapers, Larkin was a central figure in the first State Constitutional
convention.

LATHROP Possibly named after Leland Stanford's brother-in-law,
　　Avenue　　 Charles Lathrop. Leland Standford was one of the "Big
Four" who built the Central Pacific Railroad.

LATONA This is the latin word for Leto, who, in classical Greek mythol-
　　Avenue　　 ogy, was the goddess of fertility and the mother of Artemis and
Apollo. (Apollo Street is seven blocks away.)

LAURA (See Petrarch Place.)
Street

LAWTON Brigadier General Henry W. Lawton became the military gov-
　　Street　　 ernor of Santiago, Cuba after its surrender in the Spanish-
American War. In 1886, Lawton led troops into Mexico and captured
Apache Chief Geronimo. Lawton was killed in a campaign against the
insurgent leader Emilio Aguinaldo in 1909.

LECH WALESA Named to honor the Polish Solidarity leader who was
　　Street　　 awarded the Nobel Peace prize for efforts to attain
justice for his compatriots. Born of humble origins in Gdansk, this contem-
porary hero is not only the first Polish individual, but also the only Nobel

Peace prize recipient to be so honored by a street name in San Francisco. This street formerly was Ivy Street between Van Ness Avenue and Polk Street.

LE CONTE Avenue Professor John Le Conte, teacher, scientist, and author, served as the third president of the University of California. After extensive teaching in eastern colleges, Le Conte moved to Berkeley where he was chosen its first faculty member. A professor of physics, Le Conte assumed the presidency from 1869 to 1870 and again from 1875 to 1881. During his tenure, Le Conte was credited with enrouraging scientific courses and setting new entrance requirements.

LEAVENWORTH Street Rev. Thaddeu M. Leavenworth was an Episcopal minister, physician, and pharmacist, who served as an *alcalde* (chief magistrate) in 1848–49.

LEE Avenue Presumed to be named for Lieutenant Curtis Lee, a son of Robert E. Lee. Curtis Lee was an aide to General Clark who commanded the Department of California.

LEESE Street Jacob Primer Leese built the first permanent house in Yerba Buena on the block bounded by Grant, Sacramento, Clay, and Stockton Streets in 1836. Leese was a merchant and a large property holder. He married Vallejo's sister and probably because of this, was taken prisoner with Vallejo during the Bear Flag Revolt and held captive at Sutter's Fort.

LEGION OF HONOR Drive Named after the Palace of the Legion of Honor in Lincoln Park which was named after a comparable building in Paris. The original building was built by Napoleon to honor his military forces.

LEIDESDORFF Street William A. Leidesdorff, a black man, was born in the Danish West Indies and brought up by a wealthy plantation owner. In 1841, Leidesdorff arrived in San Francisco and became one of its most enterprising and public-spirited citizens. A merchant and owner of much land, Leidesdorff served as Captain of the port. He built the first hotel—The City Hotel—and was appointed Vice Consul at Yerba Buena in 1845. He also served as City Treasurer, a member of the school board, and one of the first municipal council members as well as, for a time, the Russian consul. Leidesdorff operated the first steamer on the Bay—the Russian ship *Sitka*. After his death of brain fever, Leidesdorff was buried in the Mission Dolores cemetery.

LENDRUM Court Named in honor of Captain John H. Lendrum, commanding officer of the Presidio in 1858, and the first commander of Fort Point in 1861.

LENOX Way Named possibly for the town in Massachusetts which was probably named for one of several Charles Lennoxes, Dukes of Richmond.

LEXINGTON Street Named after the city in Massachusetts where the first Revolutionary War battle was fought on April 9, 1775. Seventy-seven minutemen took their positions on the green to resist the British force of 700 men. The town was named for Lexington (now Laxton), England.

LIBERTY   After the Civil War, those naming the city's streets were
   Street   caught in a burst of patriotism and sought to find appropriate
words such as this one to express their feelings.

LICK   James Lick, an eccentic Pennsylvanian, worked his way to San
Place   Francisco via South America by selling pianos. He arrived just
before the gold rush with about $30,000. Intent on accumulating a larger
fortune, Lick invested in what was then outlying real estate. Some of his
investments included a fruit orchard in the Santa Clara valley, a flour mill
in the San Jose area, and Lick House, a famous restaurant and hotel of its
day. As a result of these ventures, Lick was very wealthy when he died; he
left several million dollars for scientific, charitable, and educational purposes. The Lick Observatory atop Mount Hamilton and the Lick Wil-
merding School in San Francisco exist because of his philanthropy.

LIGGETT   Lt. General Hunter Liggett was the commanding officer of
   Avenue   the Western Department from May 1, 1914, until September,
1917 and was commanding officer of the Ninth Corps from August, 1919
until March, 1921. This street was named in 1923.

LILLIAN   Lillian Wood was a prominent community leader in Hunters
   Street   Point during the 1960s when the Redevelopment Authority's
project was developing there.

LINARES   Named for a soldier of Anza's company of 1776.
   Avenue

   LINCOLN   Abraham Lincoln (1809–1865), sixteenth president of
Boulevard, Court,   the United States, preserved the Union during the
   and Way   American Civil War and emancipated the slaves. Of
humble origin, Lincoln was a self-educated lawyer. Although he lost a
series of debates with Stephen A. Douglas of Illinois in a run for a Senate
seat, Lincoln acquired such fame that he was able to become president.
Lincoln was assassinated by John Wilkes Booth, an actor, shortly after the
Union victory.

LINDA   In Spanish, *linda* means "pretty," but this was probably the name
   Street   of a friend of a contractor or politician.

LISBON   Named for the Portuguese capital city. The name is probably
   Street   derived from *áqua boa* or "good water."

LOBOS   In Spanish, this word literally means "wolves," but along the
   Street   California coast the word has been applied to sea lions.

LOEHR   Ferdinand Loehr was the editor of the "California Democrat" (a
   Street   German language newspaper) and also a physician who resided at
614 Sacramento Street.

LOMA VISTA   The Spanish geographical term "loma" designates a
   Terrace   low, long hill, but it is occasionally applied to higher hills
or mountains. *Vista* means "view" in Spanish. There is a view of the city
from some of the homes on this short street located on the side of a hill.

LOMBARD   Named by Jasper O'Farrell for the street of the same name in
   Street   Philadelphia which obtained its name from London's financial
street. The name is originally derived from the Italian moneylenders of

Genoa and Florence – the Lombards – who replaced the persecuted Jews in the fourteenth and fifteenth centuries. A Germanic people, the Lombards founded Lombardy in northern Italy in 568 A.D. One source asserts that these people got their name from their long, uncut beards. A block on this street between Hyde and Leavenworth Streets has been called "the crookedest street in the world." In 1923 eight turns were fashioned onto this one block of Lombard Street.

LOMITA The Mexican or Spanish diminuitive of *Loma* meaning "little
Avenue   hill." Las Lomitas was the name given to Yerba Buena by the
early Spaniards.

LONDON Named after the capital of the United Kingdom and the center
Street   of the Commonwealth of Nations. London is Great Britain's
largest port and industrial complex as well as its principal financial, commercial, and cultural center. In Roman times this city was known as Londinium.

LONE MOUNTAIN Named for the mountain, distinct and separate from
Terrace   San Francisco's other mountains.

LONGVIEW One of a series of streets in this residential subdivision which
Court   originates on Panorama Drive and which shares the suffix –
"view."

LOPEZ Named for one of the first settlers in San Francisco, a member of
Avenue the Anza party of 1776.

LOS PALMOS In Spanish, this means "the palms." At present, however
Drive   there are only three palm trees on this street. Presumably
when this street name was selected there were more such trees.

LOTTIE BENNETT An appropriate name for a street in a housing
Lane   project sponsored by the International Long-
shoremen's Union. The *Lottie Bennett* was a four-masted schooner built at Point Blakely, Washington, in 1899. She carried timber until 1924. During the next six years, she sailed the South Seas. In 1935, she was reconditioned and subsequently used in a motion picture near San Pedro. In 1937, she was finally laid up in Long Beach.

LOUISBERG Named possibly after the square on Beacon Hill. Boston,
Street   which is one of the urban design landmarks of that city.

LOWER One of two streets—the other one is Upper Terrace—on the
Terrace slopes of Mt. Olympus, whose names give a verbal sense of
their visual relationship.

LOYOLA Adjacent to the campus of the University of San Francisco, the
Terrace city's first university. This street was named for Saint Ignatius
of Loyola (1491–1556). His name comes from his home town—Loyola, Spain. Saint Ignatius became one of the most influential figures in the Catholic Reformation and founded the Society of Jesus—the Jesuits—in 1534.

LUCERNE Probably named after the lake or city in Switzerland, possi-
Street   bly the hometown of a pioneer. The name is derived from the

Benedictine monastery of St. Leodezar (Luciara) founded in the 8th century and later a cell of the Murbach monastery in Alsace.

LUM
Place
See Walter U. Lum Place.

LUNADO
Court
(Also Way) A form of the Spanish word for "moon." Our word "lunatic" is derived from the same word, *luna*. *Lunado* means crescent-shaped.

LUNDY'S
Lane
Named for the Battle of Lundy's Lane which took place on July 25, 1814. The battle, occurring a mile west of Niagara Falls, ended the United States' invasion of Canada during the War of 1812.

LURELINE
Street
The Lureline was one of the most popular tourist ships which went between San Francisco and Hawaii. The street was named after the ship in order to capitalize on the allure of the islands, and besides, it sounds nice.

LYON
Street
Captain Nathaniel Lyon graduated from West Point and fought in the Florida and Mexican Wars. In California, Lyon was actively engaged in campaigns against the Indians. He was killed in the Civil War.

MABINI
Street
Named for a Filipino theoretician and spokesman of the Philippine Revolution. Mabini wrote the Constitution for the short-lived republic which existed there in 1898–99. Prior to 1979, this street was called Alice Street.

MACARTHUR
Avenue
Lt. General Arthur MacArthur was the father of General Douglas MacArthur, a general during World War II. But Arthur MacArthur was commander of the U.S. Army in the Department of California in 1903–05 and also temporary commander of this same organization in 1907. He also served in the Civil and Spanish-American Wars, where he was awarded a Medal of Honor for bravery.

MACEDONIA
Street
Named after the central part of the Balkan penisula lying astride the frontiers of southern Yugoslavia, northern Greece, and southwest Bulgaria. The name is derived from Macedonis, the Bishop of Constantinople in the middle of the fourth century. He was deposed for suggesting a new view of the Holy Trinity. Those who accepted this somewhat heretical view were called Macedonians.

MACONDRAY
Lane
Frederick William Macondray was a son of a Scottish sea captain who arrived in San Francisco in 1849. After an early career at sea, he established the large merchantile firm of Macondray and Co.

MADERA
Street
Named for the California county which was named for the Spanish word for "wood," and it is an appropriate name for a street which ends in a park.

MADISON
Street
Probably named for James Madison (1751–1836), the fourth President of the United States and one of the founding fathers. Madison is also known as the father of the United States Constitution. Prior to serving as president, Madison was Jefferson's Secretary of State for eight years.

MADRID Named after the capital of Spain and the highest of the Euro-
    Street   pean capital cities (2,100 ft.). Named the official capital in 1607,
it was associated with a succession of Spanish kings and developed a rich
cultural and architectural heritage. The name, however, is probably
derived from an earlier time when a small Moorish fort called Majrit was
located on the site. This fort was a part of the outlying defenses of Toledo,
40 miles to the southwest.

MADRONE Named after the broad-leafed evergreen shrub or tree which
    Avenue   grows from British Columbia to southern California.

MAGELLAN Named for a member of the Portolá expedition, *not* after
    Avenue   Ferdinand Magellan, the famed explorer.

MAIDEN A local jeweler, Alfred Samuels, suggested this name, probably
    Lane   after the name of New York's jewelry center. Before 1906, it
was called Morton Alley, then Union Square Avenue, and then, in 1909,
Manila, to link it to the Dewey Monument on the square. While it was
Morton Alley, this street was the location of low class brothels or "cribs,"
thus suggesting another origin for its name.

MAIN Charles Main sailed from Boston to San Francisco via Cape Horn
    Street   on a voyage which lasted five months and one day in 1845. Main
began as a miner but soon switched to manufacturing, wholesaling, and
retailing leather saddleware, a business in which he became very successful. For several years, Main was the president and director of the Central
Railroad of San Francisco and of the Geary Street wire-rope railroad company. He was also a founder and director of the California Insurance Company and a director of several banks. Main was instrumental in securing
passage of a bill which widened Kearny Street from Market Street to
Broadway.

MAJESTIC The view from the southern end (or beginning) of this street
    Avenue   looking towards Twin Peaks and the San Francisco Bay is
           majestic.

MALLORCA Named after the Spanish island—the largest in the West-
    Way   ern Mediterranean Balearic chain.

MALTA Named for the island in the central Mediterranean Sea.
    Drive

MANCHESTER Probably named for the manufacturing city in En-
    Street   gland, named by the Romans when they built a fort on
the site of the existing city (78–86 A.D.). They named the fort
Mamucium—place of the breastlike hill—perhaps an earlier version of
San Francisco's Twin Peaks.

MANZANITA In Spanish, this means "little apple," since it is the dimin-
    Avenue   utive of *manzana*. This native shrub of California moun-
tain areas has red berries resembling apples, hence the Spanish name.

MARIN Named for Marin County, in turn named for Chief Marin of the
    Street   Licatiut Indians, a tribe of the Coastal Miwok. His name is not
Indian in origin, but is probably derived from his capture. Marin was baptized *Marinero* or "sailor" because he was an excellent navigator. Later he

was the first ferryman on San Francisco Bay. It is certainly an appropriate name for a street that parallels the Islais Creek Channel and almost runs into the Bay. (See also Marin in the Bay Area landmarks section of this book.)

MARENGO Street Named after the Battle of Marengo which took place on June 14, 1800. Here in northern Italy, Napoleon's troops narrowly defeated the Austrian army. The victory secured Napoleon's military and civilian authority in Paris. Napoleon Street is located nearby.

MARINA Boulevard This is the Spanish word for "seacoast."

MARIPOSA Street Named after the county which, in turn, was named for the Spanish word for "butterfly."

MARK Lane Mark Aldrich (1801–1873) has the distinction of being a member of a select group whose first and last names are used for two different streets in San Francisco. The other is Aldrich Alley. Although his life was colorful, no one knows why he was so honored.

MARKET Street This main thoroughfare was laid out by Jasper O'Farrell, the city's civil engineer, in 1846. He meant it to run parallel to the Old Mission trail, the first road between Yerba Buena Cove and Mission Dolores. George Hyde, another city official and a Philadelphian, may have suggested the street be named after the major east/west street in his home town. Philadelphia's Market Street was originally called High Street. By 1759, however, the name was changed because the street served the city's market. San Francisco's Market Street crosses the North of Market area at a forty-five degree angle, thus causing much confusion for motorists, pedestrians, and property owners.

MARS Street Named for the ancient Roman god, second only to Jupiter in importance. In Roman literature, Mars was god of war and protector of Rome. Also the name of a planet, Mars runs next to Uranus, itself intersecting Saturn. All are located on the slopes of Mt. Olympus.

MARSILLY Street Mrs. Roman De Boom's maiden name. The De Boom family once owned the tract of land on which this street is located.

MARTIN LUTHER KING, JR. Drive Named in December 1983 to honor the slain civil rights leader. Located in Golden Gate Park, this street is positioned between John F. Kennedy Drive and Lincoln Way. Winner of the Nobel Peace Prize in 1964 for his leadership of nonviolent resistance in the struggle for racial equality, this eloquent black Baptist minister will long be remembered for his speech "I Have A Dream" delivered in 1963 during a massive demonstration in Washington, D.C.

MARVIEW Way Literally, "a view of the sea" in Spanish/English. This is one of a number of streets in this residential subdivision whose suffix is "view."

MARY Street Named for a friend or relative of a pioneer.

MASON Street Colonel Richard B. Mason was military governor of California from May, 1847, to February, 1849. In the summer of 1848, Mason made an inspection of the gold district and sent the famous report to Washington, D.C. which, along with letters from Thomas Larkin, started the big rush to California the following year.

MASONIC Avenue This street originally ran by the Masonic cemetery which was operated by the fraternal order. The English word "mason" is from the French *Masson* which means bricklayer.

MATEO Street This word means "Matthew" in Spanish. (See San Mateo Avenue.)

MAYWOOD Drive One of a number of streets in Westwood Highlands whose suffix is "wood."

Mᶜ ALLISTER Street Hall McAllister, an attorney and distinguished jurist, was referred to as the most eminent lawyer in California during the Gold Rush period. It is said that in 1849 McAllister gave either $35 or a bottle of champagne to a city official in return for the promise of having a street named after him. He is also reputed to have gambled away his home on the toss of a single card. In 1849, McAllister won fame by having the notorius "Hounds" convicted. This was a group of former criminals who professed law and order but actually were intent on continuing their old behavior.

MᶜCARTHY Street This street may have been named for either Peter or James McCarthy. The latter is more likely. He was San Francisco's third Planning Director. In the early 1960s he worked closely with Joseph Eichler, developer of Argonaut Place which abuts this street. Peter was an early settler in Visitacion Valley where this street is situated. A newspaper distributor, his daughter, Kate, married Ted Schwerin whose father and mother both had streets named for them.

Mᶜ COPPIN Street Frank H. McCoppin was the ninth mayor of San Francisco, serving from 1867 to 1869. In 1860, McCoppin was general manager of the Old Market Street Railroad Co., which ran steam trains on Market Street, the city's first mechanical public transportation.

Mᶜ KINNON Avenue Father McKinnon was the chaplain of the First California Volunteers in the Spanish-American War. He died in the Philippines.

Mᶜ LAREN Avenue John McLaren, a Scotsman, was superintendent of Golden Gate Park for almost fifty-six years. A master horticulturist, McLaren transformed the windswept sand dunes, 1,017 acres, into the largest and most beautiful man-made park in the world. He died in his nineties in 1943.

MEADE Avenue General George G. Meade (1815–1872) played a critical role in the Civil War by leading the defeat of the Confederate Army at Gettysburg in July 1863. Meade repulsed Lee's forces with great tactical skill; however, he has been criticized by some for allowing Lee's army to escape after this decisive victory.

MELBA Probably named after Dame Nellie Melba, for whom a toast and
Court dessert were also named. She was an operatic soprano, famed
for her performances of coloratura roles in the latter part of the last century and first quarter of this one. She was born Helen Mitchell in Richmond, near Melbourne, Australia, and her stage name is derived from that
of her native town.

THOMAS MELLON Named after a distinguished civil servant who
Drive served as the city's chief administrative officer
from 1964 through 1976. Prior to this appointment, Mr. Mellon had been
president of the Chamber of Commerce. After his career in public service,
he became involved in the Executive Office Park real estate development
in which this street is located.

MENDELL Colonel George H. Mendell, of the Army Corps of En-
Street gineers, directed many Pacific Coast defenses. In San Francisco, Mendell served as president of the Board of Public Works from
1900–1903.

MENDOSA Antonio de Mendosa was the Spanish Viceroy in Mexico
Avenue City and the superior officer under whom the Coronado and
Cabrillo expeditions were made.

MERCED In Spanish, this means "mercy." "The Lady of Mercy" is the
Avenue Virgin Mary.

MERCEDES The word is derived from the Spanish word for "mercy."
Way

MERCHANT Named in honor of Brigadier General Charles S. Mer-
Street chant, who served in the War of 1812 and was twice the
commanding officer of the Presidio.

MERCURY Mercury was the Roman god of merchandise and mer-
Street chants. He is usually represented as standing and holding a
purse, symbolic of his business functions. Mercury is also the name of a
planet. This street is situated near Venus and Neptune Streets.

MERSEY Probably named after the river in England which flows past
Street Liverpool down to the Irish Sea.

MESA (Also Avenue) Named in honor of Alfrez Juan Prado Mesa, acting
Street commanding officer of the Presidio in 1835, 1839, and 1843.

MICHIGAN Named after the state – the only one of the 49 continental
Street states to be split into two large land segments, both of which
are peninsulas. The name is from an Indian word of uncertain origin. One
theory claims derivation from *mitchisawgyegan,* a combination of Indian
words meaning "great lake" (presumably Lake Michigan). Another suggests *mishi-maikin-nac,* "swimming turtle," an Indian term used to
describe the profile of the northern tip of the southern peninsula and a
nearby island. Thus, it is unclear which was named first, the lake or the land
area.

MIDCREST An appropriate name for a street which is located near the
Way top of Twin Peaks.

MIDDLE This road in Golden Gate Park lies between what was once
Drive North Drive and South Drive. Now, however, North Drive has
been renamed John F. Kennedy Drive and South Drive has been renamed
Martin Luther King, Jr. Drive. One might therefore suspect that Middle
Drive would be a good candidate for a name change.

MIDDLE POINT This street lies between West Point Road and Hunters
Road Point Road. One would think that there might be or
might have been an East Point Road, but, alas, that is not the case.

MIDWAY This street lies halfway between Stockton and Grant Streets
Street and connects Francisco Street with Bay Street.

MILAN Probably named after the city in Northern Italy, a leading fi-
Terrace nancial, industrial, and commercial center. At the time of the
Roman conquest—222 B.C.—the town was called Mediolanum.

MILEY Probably named in honor of Lieutenant Colonel John D. Miley
Street who died in Manila on September 19, 1899, during the Spanish-
American War. Fort Miley is also named for this officer.

MINERVA In the Roman religion, Minerva was the goddess of hand-
Street icraft, professions, arts, and, later, war.

MINNA Probably named for a pioneer.
Street

MINNESOTA Named after the state which was named for the river which
Street joins with the Mississippi River near the state capital of St.
Paul. The name of the river is derived from a Dakota (Sioux) Indian word.
While scholars agree that *minne* means "water," there is a difference of
opinion concerning *sota*. Most agree that *sota* refers to the reflection of the
sky upon the water but disagree as to whether *Minnesota* means "water
reflecting cloudy skies."

MINT Named because this street is adjacent to the second United States
Street branch mint in California. (The first such mint was located on
Commercial Street between Montgomery and Kearny Streets.) The build-
ing survived the earthquake and fire of 1906 and today is a museum.

MIRALOMA In Spanish, this means "hill view." Technically, however,
Drive *Mira* does not mean "view" as it is generally assumed, but
rather is an imperative meaning "look" or "behold."

MIRAMAR This word means "sea view" in Spanish. The name is a pop-
Street ular one for country homes in Spanish-speaking lands. It
was the name given, for example, to the Spanish royal chalet located at
San Sebastian on the Bay of Biscay.

MIRANDO In Spanish, *Mirando* means "looking."
Way

MISSION The longest (7.29 miles) and one of the oldest streets in San
Street Francisco, this road follows the original trail which linked the
village of Yerba Buena with Mission Dolores. Originally a toll road, it was
planked for two and one-half miles starting at Third Street.

MISSION ROCK This street lies on the approach to the Mission Rock
    Street   ship terminal, named for the large rock in what was
once called Mission Bay. (There was also a Mission Creek which fed into
the Bay.) All these places take their name from the nearby Mission
Dolores.

MISSISSIPPI Named after the state whose western border primarily is
    Street   the river of the same name. The river was named by the
Algonquian speaking Indians and they called it the "Father of Waters." It is
derived from *meeche* or *mescha* "great," and *cebe,* "river" or "water."

MISSOURI Named after the state which is bisected by the river of the
    Street   same name. The river was given its name by French explor-
ers after a neighbouring Indian tribe who inhabited an area near the mouth
of the river. On some early French maps this river was named *Peki-tan-oui*
or *Pokitanou* which means "muddy water" and later *Oomessourit.*

MIZPAH Named after the biblical town of the same name, which in He-
    Street   brew means "of Benjamin." This city is in the Israeli-occupied
part of Jordan (or central Palestine) north of Jerusalem.

MODOC This word was used by the Klamath Indians when speaking of a
    Avenue   tribe which lived south of them. It means "southerners" and is
also the name of a county in northeastern California near where the
Klamath Indians once lived.

MOJAVE Named after the desert and river of the same name. The name
    Street   is an Hispanicized phonetic rendering of the name of a Yuman
Indian tribe first called Jamajah by Franciscan missionary explorer Father
Francisco Garcés in 1775. It is more accurately rendered in English as
Hamakhava. One discredited theory is that the name was derived from the
three pinnacles now known as the needles or the three mountain ranges
surrounding the Mojave Desert. (See also Garcés Drive.)

MONCADA Fernando Rivera y Moncada was second in command to
    Way   Portolá, governor of California, from 1773 to 1777. Rivera
Street was also named for him. Moncada opposed the early settlement of
Yerba Buena (now San Francisco), preferring that new settlers expand the
small population base of the capital at Monterey. Quarrelling with De
Anza, he ordered his lieutenant, Moraga, to establish only a presidio and
not a mission. These instructions were ignored. He was killed by Yuma
Indians in 1788. (See also Garcés Drive.)

MONO Named for the Shoshone-speaking Indian tribe of Central Califor-
    Street   nia. There were two branches, the Eastern and Western, who
traded with each other. The latter group lived in the pine belt of the Sierra
Nevada, while the former lived east of the crest of this range near Mono
Lake.

MONROE Probably named after James Monroe, the fifth president of
    Street   the United States and author of the Monroe Doctrine. This
document warned European powers against interference in the Americas.

MONTALVO Named for García Ordóñez de Montalvo who was the
    Avenue   author of *Las Sèrgas de Esplandián* in which the word
"California" first appeared.

MONTECITO This word means "little mountain" in Spanish.
Avenue

MONTEREY Named after the city and county named in honor of Gaspar
Boulevard de Zuñiga, Count of Monterey and Viceroy of Mexico.
Earlier spellings of this word were Monterrey and Monte Rey.

MONTEZUMA Named after the legendary leader of the Aztecs in Mex-
Street ico during the Spanish conquest. Montezuma was the
last Aztec emperor, famous for his dramatic confrontation with the Spanish conquistador, Hernán Cortés. The adjacent street is Aztec Street.

MONTGOMERY Captain John B. Montgomery received orders from
Street Commodore Sloat to occupy the little town of Yerba
Buena for the United States on July 9, 1846. Montgomery landed seventy
men from his boat, the U.S.S. *Portsmouth*, and raised the American flag at
the Plaza amid, as one spectator later wrote, "the roar of cannon from the
ship, and hurrahs of the ship's company, the vivas of the Californians, the
cheers of the Dutchmen, the barking of dogs, braying of jackasses, and
a general confusion of sounds from every living thing within hearing."
Montgomery remained in command of the district for five months.
Along with Kearny, Washington, and Clay—the names of other streets—
Montgomery has been in continuous usage as a street name longer than
any other.

MONTICELLO Italian for "little hill." An appropriate name since this
Street street is in Merced Heights.

MORAGA (Also Street) Lieutenant José Joaquin Moraga was second in
Avenue command of the Anza expedition in 1776. Left in command at
the Presidio when building started there, he remained the first commanding officer until July 1785. Moraga also played a leading role in the construction of Mission Dolores and Santa Clara Mission as well as in establishing the town of San Jose.

MORNINGSIDE Possibly named after the thoroughfare of the same
Drive name in New York City. In turn, this street was named
for the park which it borders on the west. The park occupies the eastern or
morning side of a rocky elevation which has become a park and which acts
as Harlem's western border.

MORRIS George R. Morris operated a store in China Camp in the 1850s
Street and 1860s. He died defending his business during a robbery.

MOSCOW Named after the capital and largest city of the Soviet Union –
Street Moskva, which lies on the river of the same name.

MOSS J. Mora Moss (1807–1880) came to San Francisco in 1850 from his
Street native Philadelphia. Moss soon was affiliated with the banking
firm of Pioche and Bayesque and the Alaska Fur Company. He was the
first president and major stockholder of the San Francisco Gas Company.
A member of the Board of Directors of the Deaf and Dumb Asylum, Moss
was elected an honorary regent of the University of California in 1868 and
was reappointed in March 1874 for a full term.

MOULTRIE Named after the fort in Charleston, South Carolina, which
Street   in turn was named to honor William Moultrie, a native of
that area who resisted the British incursions into the South during the
War of Independence. After the war, he served two terms as governor of
his state.

MT. SUTRO Named after the mountain which in turn was named for
Drive   Adolph Sutro, the twenty-first mayor of San Francisco.
(See Sutro Heights Avenue.)

MOUNT VERNON Probably named after the home and burial place of
Avenue   George Washington in Fairfax County, Virginia, on
the Potomac River, 15 miles southeast of Washington, D.C. The homesite
was named by Washington's older brother, Lawrence, to honor his former
commander, Admiral Edward Vernon, under whom he had served in the
Caribbean.

MOUNTAIN SPRING An appropriate name for a street on the edge of
Avenue   Twin Peaks.

MOUNTAIN VIEW With a view of Twin Peaks, this is an appropriate
Court   name for this street, one of a number in this residential subdivision whose suffix is "view."

JOHN MUIR John Muir was a famous naturalist and conservationist
Drive   who founded the Sierra Club in 1892. A native of Scotland,
he spent his boyhood on a Wisconsin farm before moving to the West.
Muir explored parts of the Yosemite Valley and Upper Sierra. He led a
successful campaign to have the valley taken over by the United States as
a national park.

MUNICH Named after the third largest German city and the capital and
Street   largest city of Bavaria. The German word for this city is
München which means "Home of the Monks."

MURRAY Named for one of the teachers at St. Mary's College, founded
Street   in 1863, when it was located in San Francisco.

MUSEUM The museum is the J.D. Randall Junior Museum—this road
Way   leads to it.

NANTUCKET Named after the island situated 25 miles off Cape
Avenue   Cod, Massachusetts, and 15 miles east of Martha's
Vineyard. The name is Indian for "far away land."

NAPIER Here one finds the last wooden sidewalk and some of the oldest
Lane   houses in San Francisco. Legend has it that in these homes
sailors were drugged, kidnapped, and put onto vessels for crew. Who
Napier was remains a mystery.

NAPLES Named after the Italian city which is called Napoli today, but
Street   which in ancient times was called Neapolis, or New Town. In
Greek *polis* means "town" or "city." From the middle ages to 1860, Napoli
was the capital of the Kingdom of Naples which occupied the southern portion of the Italian peninsula.

NAPOLEON Named after Napoleon Bonaparte the French general and
Street emperor (1769–1821). One of the most celebrated person-
ages in the history of the West, he temporarily extended French domination over a large part of Europe leaving a lasting mark on the lands he
ruled. Waterloo Street is nearby, (see also Legion of Honor Drive).

NATICK Probably named after the town in Scotland which was the
Street home of Allen of Allen Street.

NATOMA Named after an Indian tribe on the American and Feather
Street rivers in the vicinity of Natomas. The Indian name has several
translations; one version gives it as "the girl from the mountains" while
another suggests direction and is interpreted as "up-stream."

NAUTILUS Probably named after the mollusk or the chambered ma-
Street chine of Oliver Wendell Holmes' poetic fancy.

NAVAJO Named after the tribe, currently the most populous of all Indian
Avenue groups in the United States with about 100,000 individuals
scattered throughout northwestern New Mexico, northeastern Arizona,
and southeastern Utah.

NAVY This is a secondary approach road to the naval shipyards at Hunt-
Road ers Point and a thoroughfare within it; aptly, if not imaginatively,
named.

NEBRASKA Named after the state. The name is derived from an Indian
Street word meaning "flat water" – a reference to both the Platte
and Nebraska rivers. The Omaha Indian name is *Niubthatka*; the Oto is
Nebrathka.

NEPTUNE In Roman mythology, Neptune was the god of fresh water,
Street therefore not a sea god; however, he is usually considered as
such. This is one of a series of streets in the Bay View district named after
Roman gods. Also the name of a planet, Neptune is near Venus and Saturn
Streets.

NEVADA Named after the state. The word is a shortened form of *Sierra*
Street *Nevada*, a mountain range in western Nevada along the
California border, named for the range in southern Spain. In Spanish *sierra*
means "mountain range," and *nevada* means "snow-covered."

NEW MONTGOMERY This was originally a privately constructed
Street street—largely for the benefit of the Palace and
Grand hotels. It was built by William Ralston and a friend, Asbury Harp-
ending, at their own expense in 1868 and 1869. They had private plans to
extend it from Howard Street to South Park and Rincon Hill, and from
there on to the Bay. It was named after Montgomery Street and was originally called Montgomery Street South.

NEWHALL Henry M. Newhall, a native of Massachusetts, came to Cali-
Street fornia in 1849. In San Francisco, Newhall was a leading real
estate auctioneer, then a large buyer of real estate himself. He founded the
town which bears his name in Southern California. A scion of the Newhall
clan, Scott Newhall, began his professional career as a photographer and
spent his last eighteen years (1953–1971) as editor and executive editor of
the *San Francisco Chronicle*.

NEWBURG   A short street possibly named for the city in New York or
   Street   Scotland. *Burg* means "town" in German, and hence this
name means a new town.

NEWCOMB   Simon Newcomb (1835–1909) was a distinguished astron-
   Avenue   omer and mathematician who prepared ephemerides—
locations of celestial bodies over a period of time—and tables of astro-
nomical constants which are still in use.

NIAGARA   Named after the river and world-renowned falls constitut-
   Avenue   ing a part of the boundary between the United States and
   Canada.

NIANTIC   Named after the sailing vessel *Niantic*, built about 1835 and
   Avenue   captained by Robert Bennett Forbes, one of the most distinguished figures in nautical America in the 19th century. Forbes learned
about the Gold Rush while in Payta, Peru, and took his whaling ship to
Panama. Here he loaded it up with several hundred Argonauts and delivered them to San Francisco, where the ship was hauled ashore and made
into a combination office building, hotel, and storeship. All the upper
works burned in the great fire of May 1851. The bottom was discovered
during the excavation of a highrise at the corner of Clay and Sansome
streets in 1978.

NIDO   This is the Spanish word for "nest;" it is often used in the applied
Avenue   sense of "home."

NIMITZ   Admiral Chester Nimitz was the naval commander of the U.S.
   Drive   Pacific Fleet in World War II (1885–1966). Nimitz is acknowledged as one of the navy's foremost administrators and strategists. He
exercised authority over all land and sea forces in the Pacific area. This
street is appropriately named since it abuts the Hunters Point Naval Ship-
yard where many navy vessels were repaired during the war.

NOB HILL   See Nob Hill in the Bay Area Landmarks section.
   Circle

NOE   José Noé was the last *alcalde* (chief magistrate) under Mexican
Street   rule, and a city official after the American occupation. Noé owned
a ranch of approximately 4,000 acres in the center of present-day San
Francisco. He is buried in the Mission Dolores Cemetery.

NORFOLK   Probably named after the hometown of one of the pioneers.
   Street   The Nebraskan city on the north fork of the Elkhorn river
owes its name to the abbreviation of North Fork. Norfolk, Virginia, is
named after the English county located north of Suffolk, again suggesting
an abbreviation of a geographical fact.

NORIEGA   Named for José de la Guerra y Noriega (1792–1870), com-
   Street   mander of Monterey and Santa Barbara. Founder of a great
family, Noriega was an *alcalde* of San Jose and fought in the Bear Flag
Revolt.

NORMANDIE   Named after the French province or district, named in
   Terrace   turn for the Normans. They settled in what became

known as the Duchy of Normandy. Their name is derived from the term *Nortmanni* or "Northmen" because they were of Viking stock.

NORTH POINT Street Named after the north point, once jutting into the Bay near this street.

NORTH VIEW Court Named for the fact that a view to the north and towards the Bay is afforded from this short street.

NORTHGATE Drive You won't find a north gate at this northern entrance to Mount Davidson Manor. In the 1920s, when this sub-division was built, this name suggested exclusivity and security.

NORTHRIDGE Road Named for the location on the north ridge of the hill which extends towards Hunters Point.

NORTHWOOD Drive All of the streets in Westwood Park end in "wood." As might be expected, this is the northernmost street.

NORWICH Street Probably named after the city in England. The original name for this Saxon settlement was Northwic.

NOTTINGHAM Place Probably named after the town in England. The original site was occupied by the Anglo-Saxons in the 6th century. They bestowed on their settlement the name of Snotingaham—the "ham" or village of Snot's people.

NUEVA Avenue This is Spanish for "new."

O'FARRELL Street Philadelphian Jasper O'Farrell was the civil engineer chosen to revise the street survey made in 1839 by Jean Jacques Vioget. His maps covered the area bounded by Post, Leavenworth, and Francisco Streets, and the Bay. O'Farrell corrected Vioget's street angles, which were 2½ degrees off right angles, and extended the city's streets in all directions. Some of his maps, however, were reported to have caused a civic demonstration. He laid out Market Street, and the property owners protested both the diagonal mapping and the length which at that time extended far into the country. Now motorists—as well as property owners—continue to protest the difficulties created by the diagonal swath of Market Street in the midst of a gridiron arrangement of other streets.

O'SHAUGHNESSY Boulevard Michael Maurice O'Shaughnessy arrived in San Francisco from his native Ireland at the age of 21 in 1885. In the years that followed, O'Shaughnessy built dams, aqueducts, bridges, and railroads from one end of the Pacific Coast to the other, as well as Hawaii and the distant Eastern cities. For 22 years, O'Shaughnessy served as San Francisco's chief engineer, building tunnels, boulevards, and the municipal streetcar system. O'Shaughnessy was responsible for the Hetch Hetchy water/sewer system, which brings water to San Franciscans from the Sierra Nevada mountains.

OAK GROVE Street There may have been an oak grove here at one time, but now all one finds above this tiny alley is the Bay Bridge freeway approach.

OAK PARK   Situated in Forest Knolls subdivision where all the streets
   Drive   have a "woodsy" ring. Although bottlebrush pines may be
seen, no oaks are visible.

OAKHURST   Situated in Forest Knolls subdivision where all the streets
   Lane   have a "woodsy" ring, this street has yet to be developed.

OCEAN   Originally Ocean House Road; the house in question was located
 Avenue   near the Pacific Ocean.

OCTAVIA   Miss Octavia Gough, sister to Charles Gough, was a member
  Street   of a committee to lay out and name streets in the Western
Addition in 1855. (See Gough Street.)

OLD CHINATOWN   The name says it all.
     Lane

OLMSTEAD   Frederic Law Olmstead (1822-1903) was one of America's
   Street   first and greatest landscape architects. He helped design
Central Park in New York and Golden Gate Park in San Francisco.

OLYMPIA   Named after the area in Greece, an ancient religious sanc-
   Way   tuary, the location of the first Olympic games. Since this road
leads to a recreation center, it would appear to be appropriately named.

ONEIDA   Named after the North American Indian tribe, one of the origi-
 Avenue   nal five nations of the Iroquois League. They lived in what is
now central New York.

ONONDAGA   Named after the North American Indian tribe which was
  Avenue   one of the original five nations of the Iroquois League. In
their native Iroquoian tongue, their name means "on the mountain."

OPHIR   Possibly named after the gold mine in Nevada owned by William
 Alley   Ralston.

ORA   Mrs. Elmer (Ora) Robinson was the wife of San Francisco's thirty-
 Way   third mayor who served in office for two four-year terms starting in
1948. Her husband also had a street named for him—hence the Robinsons
are unique, since they are the only couple in San Francisco with this distinction.

ORBEN   Bert Orben, an architect, inspired the area's redevelopment in
 Place   the 1970s by acquiring and restoring the houses along this street.
These homes were built originally in the 1880s when the street was called
Middle Street.

ORD   (Also Court) Major General Edward Ord was commanding officer
Street at the Presidio on two occasions in 1856. He later commanded the
Department of California (1868-1871). Fort Ord, near Monterey, was also
named for him.

ORIOLE   Named after the passerine bird native to the Americas.
  Way

ORTEGA   José Francesco de Ortega, a Portolá expedition scout, discov-
  Street   ered Carquinez Straits and San Francisco Bay in November
1769. Later, Ortega was commander of the Presidios of San Diego and
Monterey as well as the one at Santa Barbara, which he founded. He

also helped to found the Missions of San Juan Capistrano and San Buenaventura.

OSAGE Named after the North American Indian tribe of Sioux linguistic
Alley   stock. The Osage migrated westward from the Atlantic Ocean to their lands in what is now Oklahoma.

OSCAR Probably named for a pioneer.
Alley

OSCEOLA Osceola Washington was a prominent community leader at
Lane   Hunters Point when the Redevelopment Authority's project was planned there during the 1960s.

OTIS James Otis, twelfth mayor of San Francisco, was born in Boston. In
Street 1848, Otis was a member of the importing and exporting firm of Macondray and Company. Otis died while serving as mayor, on November 4, 1875.

OTTAWA Named after the Algonquian-speaking Indian tribe whose ter-
Avenue   ritory included what are now parts of the Ottawa River, the French River, Georgian Bay, Northern Michigan, and adjacent areas.

OVERLOOK Situated in Golden Gate Park, this thoroughfare looks over
Drive   very little other than a grove of hydrangeas. It is no longer open to vehicular traffic.

OXFORD Named after the British town and/or university. It is probable
Street   that this name was derived from the district of Oxfordshire which in turn received its name from the River Ock flowing through the area.

PACHECO In 1776, Juan Salvio Pacheco was a soldier in Anza's
Street   company, hence one of the founders of San Francisco.

PACIFIC Named after the ocean, originally called *Mar del Sur* ("South
Avenue   Sea") by its discoverer, Vasco Nuñez de Balboa, in 1513. Its current name was given to it by Magellan some time after he passed through the Straits of Magellan in November 1570. Magellan called it *El Mar Pacifico* — possibly reflecting the transition from the turbulent waters around Cape Horn. Pacific Avenue was originally called Bartlett Street in honor of Washington Bartlett, the city's first Chief Judge.

PAGE Robert C. Page was the clerk to the Board of Aldermen from 1851
Street to 1856.

PAGODA An appropriate name for one of the shortest thoroughfares in
Place   Chinatown.

PALM Named after the Royal and other varieties of palms gracing this
Avenue street.

PALO ALTO The English translation of this Spanish name means "high
Avenue   tree." The city to the south received this name after Leland Stanford's farm of the same name, named for a tall redwood tree that stood nearby. In this case, the street is appropriately named since it is situated near the top of Mount Sutro.

PALOMA After the Spanish word for "pigeon."
Avenue

PALOS In Spanish, this word means "sticks, logs, timber, or masts," but
Place   it was used in Spanish California to denote "trees."

PALOU Fray Francisco Palóu, a Franciscan padre with Anza's party,
Avenue   took a leading role in establishing both the Presidio and Mission
Dolores in 1776. Palóu had previously accompanied an exploratory expedition which placed a cross on Point Lobos above Seal Rocks in 1774.

PANAMA Named after the clipper ship *Panama* which brought some of
Street   the Forty-Niners to San Francisco. The vessel's name was
taken from the Central American country whose name means "many fish"
in an Indian language. Many Forty-Niners passed through Panama's jungles on their way to the Gold Rush.

PANORAMA This name was selected to describe the sweep and breadth
Drive   of the view that is available from this street.

PARADISE Perhaps the person who named this street believed it was
Avenue   not only a privilege to live in San Francisco, but also a paradise to live on this short street which now ends at a playground.

PARAISO This word means "paradise" in Spanish.
Place

PARAMOUNT Literally in Greek/French, "beside the mountain." This
Terrace   is not an inappropriate name for this little cul-de-sac
which is located near Lone Mountain.

PARIS Named after the capital of France which was named for the Greek
Street   God of the same name. Paris, a shepherd, was the son of King
Priam of Troy. He awarded a golden apple to Aphrodite in a contest to
determine who was the "fairest" woman in the land. The losers, Hera and
Athene, avenged themselves by bringing devastation to his country, to his
family and to Paris, himself.

PARK Probably named for the fact that this street runs to and from Holly
Street   Park.

PARK HILL Adjacent to Buena Vista Park and on a hill; therefore, this
Avenue   street was named after its lofty location.

PARKRIDGE An appropriate name for a street near the top of Twin
Drive   Peaks, although there are more apartment houses than
parkland to be seen.

PARNASSUS This street is on the slope of Mt. Sutro and was probably
Avenue   named after Mount Parnassus in Greece. This was a revered spot in Greek mythology. Apollo had his sanctuary nearby. The
mountain contained sacred caves.

PARROTT John Parrott came to San Francisco in 1848 and was a ship-
Alley   ping merchant as well as a leading banker. Parrott built one
of the city's first large buildings on the northwest corner of California and
Montgomery Streets.

PASADENA Named after the southern California city, whose name
Street   in the Chippewa Indian language means "crown of the
valley."

PENINSULA A short street going north and south in the same direction
Avenue   as the San Francisco peninsula.

PENNSYLVANIA After the state which was named for Admiral Sir
Avenue   William Penn (1621-1670), father of William Penn
(1644-1718), founder of the state which was named by Charles II of
England. Through his connections with the crown Penn secured a large
tract of land in America. He spent much of his life there developing a colony
organized according to his Quaker religious beliefs and political principles.
There is a double meaning to the name since, as Penn himself acknowledged, *penn* is a Welsh word meaning "head" or "headland" and, when
combined with *sylvania,* a Latinized word for "woodlands," the meaning is
"head woodlands" or, more clearly, "high woodlands." The name is
generally assumed to mean "Penn's woods." There is also, of course, the
famed Pennsylvania Avenue in Washington, D.C.

PERALTA Gabriel Peralta, a corporal in Anza's company, arrived in San
Avenue   Francisco with his four sons in 1776. When the United
States took over California in 1846, the Peraltas were the owners of a
49,000- acre ranch covering what is now Berkeley, Alameda, and
Oakland.

PERRY Doctor Alexander Perry was a major and a surgeon in Colonel
Street   Jonathan Stevenson's First New York Volunteer regiment, arriving in northern California in 1847.

PERSHING General John Joseph Pershing was the commanding general
Drive   of the American forces in Europe during World War I. Pershing was the first since George Washington to be appointed General of
the Armies.

PERSIA Named after the country (now Iran). The name originated from a
Avenue   region in the southern part of this country formerly known as
Persis, alternatively known as Pars or Parsa. During the rule of the Persian
Achaemid dynasty (559-330 B.C.) the ancient Greeks first encountered
the inhabitants of Pars on the Iranian Plateau, and the name was extended.

PERU Named after the country which was probably named for the region
Avenue of Piura.

PETRARCH Petrarch—scholar, poet, and humanist—is best remem-
Place   bered for poems addressed to his lover, Laura. These
works inspired much of the Renaissance flowering of lyric peotry in Italy,
France, Spain and England. There is also a Laura Street, a number of
blocks to the southwest of this street.

PHELAN James Phelan, a native of Ireland, arrived in San Francisco in
Avenue   1849. Phelan was a millionaire industrialist and banker. He
established the First National Bank of San Francisco and was its first
president. His son, James D. Phelan, became one of the city's most popular mayors and a United States senator.

PHELPS Timothy Guy Phelps, a New Yorker, arrived in San Francisco
   Street   in 1849. He had a varied career. First, Phelps was engaged in
real estate activities, then, was elected to the California legislature on the
state's first Republican ticket in 1856. Finally, Phelps was appointed Collector of Customs for San Francisco in 1869.

PHOENIX Named after the mythical bird that, like San Francisco, arose
   Terrace   reborn from the ashes. It is the city's symbol and appears on
its flag and seal. Contrary to popular opinion, however, the phoenix does
not symbolize San Francisco's rebirth after the fire of 1906, but rather
commemorates the many deadly fires of the Gold Rush era.

PICO Pio Pico served as the last Mexican governor of California in.
 Avenue 1845–46. Los Angeles also has a Pico Street.

PIEDMONT Literally, this word means "foot of the mountain" in Italian
   Street   and is an appropriate name for this street lying at the base
of Mt. Olympus.

PIERCE Franklin Pierce (1804–1869) fourteenth president of the United
   Street   States, acquired almost 30,000 square miles of land from Mexico so that a southerly route to California could be developed. Pierce's
term in office was affected by raging sectional controversy over slavery.

PILGRIM The Pilgrims were the settlers of Plymouth, Massachusetts,
 Avenue the first permanent colony in New England, in 1620. They
were not known, however, as Pilgrims until two centuries later when a
manuscript of Governor William Bradford was discovered. This document referred to the "saints" who had left Holland as "pilgrimes" from
the word "pilgrimage."

PINE There are at least two versions of the origin of this street's name.
 Street The first suggests that it was named after a downtown Philadelphia street by San Francisco's first civil engineer, Jean Jacques Vioget, a
Swiss sailor and surveyor. The other version suggests that Isaac B. Pine,
an early California pioneer, was the origin. Pine, born on July 7, 1830, in
New York, arrived in San Francisco by boat on January 4, 1848. He went
directly to the gold mines where, in addition to prospecting, he constructed dams, ditches, and flumes. In 1864, Pine was superintendent of
the Eagle Quartz mines in Amador County, an operation he was identified
with for about twenty years. His mining career also took him to British
Columbia, Nevada, and Arizona.

PINTO Pablo Pinto, born in 1732 at Villa de Sinaloa, brought his wife and
 Avenue four children with him to northern California on the Anza expedition of 1776.

PIOCHE Financier Francis Pioche is regarded as one of the city's great
  Street   builders. He was a partner in the mercantile firm of Pioche and
Bayerehque, first located on Clay Street near Portsmouth Square and
later at Jackson and Montgomery streets.

PIXLEY Frank Pixley was a pioneer with several careers. One of the
  Street   first editors of *The Argonaut*, a well-known San Francisco
newspaper, Pixley, a prominent Republican, was elected city attorney in

1850. Eight years later, he was elected to the State Assembly. In 1869, President Grant appointed him California's district attorney.

PIZARRO Probably named after Francisco Pizarro (1475–1541), who
Way accompanied Balboa on his discovery of the Pacific Ocean.
Pizarro helped conquer the Inca Empire of Peru; he consolidated Spanish power there and founded Lima.

THE PLAZA In Spanish, this means "square," which usually means
and Street a town's center of activity. Not really descriptive of
this particular plaza, but perhaps the developer had hoped that such would be the case.

PLEASANT Mary Ellen (Mammy) Pleasant (1814?–1904), a black who
Street came to San Francisco about 1849, ran a boarding and
bawdy house, using her money to aid runaway slaves and other struggling blacks. In the course of time, she became the housekeeper of a local banker, Thomas Bell, whom she apparently dominated and whose house she turned into a "House of Mystery." A small park on Bell's property is named for her. *Mammy Pleasant* by Helen Holdredge was written about her.

PLYMOUTH Probably named after the city in Massachusetts, the site of
Avenue the first permanent settlement by Europeans in New Eng-
land. It was named for the city in England from which these settlers, the Pilgrims, departed. In turn, this town's name was derived from the fact that it was situated at the mouth of the Plym river estuary.

POINT LOBOS In Spanish, *lobos* means "wolves," but along the Califor-
Avenue nia coast the word has been applied to seals and sea
lions. This street is named for the fact that it goes to and from Point Lobos, a spot close to Seal Rock where sea lions often sun-bathe.

POLARIS Located on the slope of San Bruno Mountain and running in a
Way northwesterly/southeasterly direction, this street is named
after the North Star at the end of the Little Dipper.

POLK James K. Polk, eleventh president of the United States. Under his
Street leadership, the United States acquired vast territories along the
Pacific Coast and in the Southwest. Today, this land is divided into Texas, New Mexico, Oregon, and California. In his last message to Congress, he gave the official imprimatur to the wild, but true, tales of gold in California.

POMONA Probably named for the Roman goddess of tree fruit.
Street

PONTIAC Probably named after the Ottawa Indian Chief who became
Alley one of America's greatest intertribal leaders. He organized a
combined resistance to the British takeover in the Great Lakes area after the British victory in the French and Indian war (1754–63). This name is somewhat incongruous since this street is located in Chinatown.

POPE Major General John Pope was commander of the military district
Street of the Pacific and the Department of California from 1883 to 1886.
Pope was in charge of the survey of the Pacific Railway.

PORTOLA (Also Drive) Gaspar de Portolá was the first Spanish gover-
    Street   nor of California. In 1769, Portolá marched north from San
Diego in command of the first party of Europeans to see San Francisco
Bay.

POST Merchant Gabriel B. Post came to San Francisco in 1847 and was
Street one of the city's early civic leaders. In 1849, Post became a member of the town council; later he was elected a state senator.

POTRERO This is the Spanish word for "pasture" or "cattle ground."
    Street   The area through which this street goes had just such a func-
tion in San Francisco's early days.

POWELL Doctor William J. Powell was a popular surgeon on the U.S.
    Street   war sloop, *Warren*. This vessel was active during the conquest
of California and remained in San Francisco's harbor long after. Charles
Lyman, a surveyor working on the map of San Francisco in 1847, lived in
the same house as Powell, who had established a "sanitorium" for sick
sailors ashore. Undoubtedly Lyman suggested that this street be named
for Powell.

POWHATTAN Named after a confederacy of at least 30 Algonquian-
    Avenue   speaking Indian tribes who occupied most of what is
now tidewater Virginia, the eastern shore of the Chesapeake Bay, and
possibly southern Maryland. The confederacy was formed by a powerful chief known to the English settlers as Powhattan, the father of
Pocahontas.

PRADO In Spanish, this word means "meadow."
Street

PRAGUE Named after the capital of Czechoslovakia and that nation's
    Street   leading cultural and economic center.

PRECITA Named after the adjacent park whose name means "con-
    Avenue   demned to Hell" in Spanish.

PRENTISS Possibly named for Benjamin M. Prentiss, a Union General
    Street   during the Civil War. He commanded the Sixth Division,
Army of the Tennessee, at Shiloh where he was captured. After his release, he commanded the east military district in Arkansas. When the
hostilities stopped, Prentiss practiced law.

PRESIDIO (Also Boulevard, and Terrace) In Spanish, this means
    Avenue   "garrison" or "fortified barracks." These streets were named
for the fact that they lead to, from, or are adjacent to this military installation founded by the Spanish in 1776.

PRINCETON Named after the university which in turn took its name
    Street   from the borough and township in which it is situated.
This community was renamed to honor William III, Prince of Orange-
Nassau, in 1724. This is one of a series of streets in this part of the city that
was named for a college or university.

PUEBLO This is the Spanish word for "town."
Street

PUTNAM Named for either Arthur Putnam, a famous San Francisco
Street   sculptor, who lived here around the 1860s or more probably for
General Israel Putnam (1718-1790) who fought in the Battles of Lexington,
Concord, and Bunker Hill. He was most known, however, for his unsuc-
cessful attempt to capture Havana in 1762.

QUARRY This road passes through an old quarry.
Road

QUESADA Gonzalo Ximinez de Quesada was the Spanish conqueror of
Avenue   New Granada.

QUICKSTEP An appropriate name for a street in a housing project
Lane   sponsored by the International Longshoremen's Union
since the *Quickstep* was a three-masted barkentine. Built in 1884 by S.B.
Peterson, it was put afloat in 1900, but abandoned at sea on November 24,
1904.

QUINCY Probably named after the city in Massachusetts, named in
Street   honor of John Quincy, a prominent local resident. John Quincy
Adams and his father, John Adams, both presidents of the United States,
were born and are buried here.

QUINT Leander Quint, a native of New Hampshire, came to California
Street   with a law degree in 1849. After working in the mines, Quint
opened a law practice in Sonora. He was later elected a judge in Tuolumne
County. Quint came to San Francisco in 1865 where he practiced law until
his death in 1890.

QUINTARA Probably named for an old Spanish family by the Parkside
Street   Realty Company which developed this area around the turn
             of the century.

RACCOON Probably named after the English 16-gun war sloop
Drive   *Raccoon,* which scraped bottom off the Northern California coast in 1814 and limped into the Bay for repairs. The vessel,
of course, was named after the familiar animal with short legs,
pointed nose, small erect ears and a bushy tail. Curiously, there are
probably more raccoons in San Francisco today than at any other
time in the city's history, including the centuries before the Gold
Rush when the area was largely barren of flora and fauna.

RACINE Probably named after the city and county in Wisconsin whose
Lane   name is derived from the French word for "root."

RALEIGH Possibly named after Sir Walter Raleigh (1554–1618), an Eng-
Avenue   lish adventurer, favorite of Queen Elizabeth I, and an early
American colonist.

RALSTON (Also Street) William Chapman Ralston was born in Plym-
Avenue   outh, Ohio in 1826. As a young man, Ralston sailed to San
Francisco by way of Panama. During his lifetime, he was one of the city's
foremost bankers, industrialists, and civic leaders. Ralston built the Palace Hotel, and founded the Bank of California with D.O. Mils. He died in a
drowning accident at the age of 49. His biography is entitled *The Man
Who Built San Francisco* only a slight exaggeration.

RANKIN Ira P. Rankin was a well-known pioneer. Born in Hampshire
Street   County, Massachusetts, in 1817, Rankin left for San Francisco
by way of Panama in May, 1852. After success as a merchant, he went into
the foundry business. President Lincoln appointed Rankin as collector of
the Port. Rankin ran unsuccessfully for Congress and also held a number
of civic positions such as president of the Chamber of Commerce, president of the Mercantile Library, and trustee of Lick College and the College
of California.

RAUSCH Named for Joseph N. Rausch, a Forty-Niner.
Street

RAVENWOOD One of a series of streets in Westwood Highlands which
Drive   have the same suffix.

RAYCLIFF Named for Milton S. Ray, founder of the Ray Burner Com-
Terrace   pany. He was also a well-known ornithologist and poet. He
was a curator and director of the Pacific Museum of Ornithology and lived
near where this street runs into Broadway.

RED ROCK Named after the hill around which this street winds.
Way

REDONDO This is the Spanish word for "round."
Street

REED Named after one of the survivors of the Donner party, a group of
Street   immigrants who unsuccessfully tried to cross the Sierra Nevada
mountains in 1847.

REGENT Possibly named after the street of the same name in London.
Street

RENO Possibly named after the city in Nevada near the base of the Si-
Place   erra Nevada mountains. Ths city was named for General Jessie
Lee Reno of Virginia, a Union officer who was killed in the Civil War.

REPOSA *Reposa* means "rest" in Spanish.
Way

RESERVOIR Named for the reservoir which was on this site until the mid
Street   1860s. It belonged to the San Francisco Water Company
which was absorbed by the Spring Valley Water Company in 1864.

RETIRO *Retiro* means "seclusion" in Spanish.
Way

REUEL Reuel Brady was a prominent community leader in Hunters
Court   Point during the 1960s when the Redevelopment Authority's
project there was under construction.

REVERE Named for Paul Revere, folk hero of the American Revolution.
Avenue   His dramatic horseback ride on the night of April 18, 1775,
warning Boston area residents that the British were coming was immor-
talized in a poem by Henry Wadsworth Longfellow.

REX This is the Latin word for "king."
Avenue

REY Jacques J. Rey was a lithographer at 533 Commercial Street in the
Avenue   1860s and '70s.

RHINE Named after the major waterway of the European continent. Ris-
Street   ing in the Alps, this river flows north and west for 820 miles,
passing through six countries before emptying into the North Sea.

RHODE ISLAND Named for the state, but the origin of this name is un-
Street   certain since there are two contending theories. The
island (now called Aquidneck Island) may have been the one sighted by the
Italian exploreer Giovanni di Verrazano in 1524, which he said was about
the size of the island of Rhodes in the Dodecanese Islands off the west coast
of Asia Minor. Certainly the island was seen by the Dutch explorer Adraien
Block who named it *Roodt Eylandt*, "red island." Early English settlers
used the Indian name, Aquidneck Island, until 1644 when it was changed to
the "Isle of Rhodes." The colony was called "Rhode Island and the
Providence Plantations."

RICHARDSON William A. Richardson was one of the first inhabitants of
Avenue   Yerba Buena (now San Francisco) in 1835. He drew the
first map of the town. Later, Richardson became captain of the port and
bought a large ranch, now Sausalito. Richardson Bay near this community
was also named for him.

RICO *Rico* means "rich" in Spanish.
Way

RILEY Brigadier General Bennet Riley was a native of Maryland who
Avenue   became military governor of California in 1849. Lacking Con-
gressional authority for governing the newly-acquired territory, Riley issued a proclamation calling for election of delegates to a State convention,
which drafted a constitution for what later became the state.

RINCON In Spanish, this means "corner." The southerly point of Yerba
Street   Buena harbor was originally called Rincon Point.

RINGOLD This street is named in honor of Lieutenant Cadwalader Rin-
Street   gold, a member of the first U.S. expedition in the Pacific in
1841. Ringold commanded the *U.S.S. Porpoise* and led a survey mapping
the Sacramento River as far as Colusa; he also surveyed parts of San
Francisco Bay.

RIO This is the Spanish word for "river."
Court

RIO VERDE This is Spanish for "green river."
Street

RIVAS Señora Maria Gertrudis Rivas was the wife of Ignacio Linares, a
Avenue   veteran soldier in the Anza party which came to San Francisco
in 1776. She accompanied her husband and brought her four children
with her.

RIVERA See Moncada Street.
Street

RIVOLI Named, perhaps, after the street of the same name in Paris.
Street

RIZAL The father of the Philippines was José Rizal y Mercado
Street   (1861–1896), a physician and man of letters. His life and literary
works were an inspiration to the Philippine nationalist movement.

ROANOKE Probably named after the city in Virginia or the river which
  Street flows from southwest Virginia to Albemarle Sound, North
Carolina. Another possible origin is the island on which the first child of
English parents in the New World was born (Virginia Dare, August 18,
1587). In any event, this word is the Indian term for "shell money."

ROBERT KIRK Named after the clothing store adjacent to this alley.
  Lane

ROBIN HOOD Named after the famed English rebel of Nottingham For-
  Drive est. He was the hero of a series of English ballads, some of
which date from the 14th century. Many of the most striking episodes in
the tales describe him and his companions as robbing and killing wealthy
representatives of authority. The street is located in a subdivision known
as Sherwood Forest.

ROBINSON Elmer Robinson was San Francisco's thirty-third mayor
  Drive from 1948 to 1956. A native San Franciscan, Robinson was
admitted to the State Bar in 1915. Before running for mayor, Robinson was
appointed to the muncipal court where he became a Superior Court Judge.
A Republican, he was responsible for the city's first attempt at urban
renewal. His wife also had a street named for her. The Robinsons are
unique since they are the only San Francisco couple with this distinction.
This street is adjacent to a street named for the thirty-second mayor of
San Francisco, Rodger Lapham.

ROCKRIDGE This is an appropriate name for a street situated at the top
  Drive of Sunset Heights and adjacent to Cragmont Avenue.

ROLPH James Rolph, Jr. served as mayor of San Francisco for nineteen
  Street consecutive years (1911–1930) before becoming governor of
California in 1931. He died in this office three years later. During "Sunny
Jim's" mayoral term, San Francisco emerged as a modern city. When he
took office, the city was recovering from the effects of the 1906 fire and
earthquake. By the time he left office, the civic center had been planned
with the city hall and auditorium completed.

ROME Named after the capital city of Italy. According to a Roman fable
  Street Romulus and Remus, twin sons of the God Mars, were abandoned
on the flooding Tiber River and deposited by the receding waters at the foot
of the Palantine, one of the major hills of Rome. Suckled by a she-wolf, they
were reared by a shepherd and grew up to found Rome – to which Romulus
gave his name.

ROOSEVELT Since this street acquired its name in the mid-twenties, it
  Way was probably named for Theodore Roosevelt, the twenty-
sixth president of the United States. He was also a writer, explorer, and
soldier. He was elected vice president in 1900 and succeeded McKinley
when he was assassinated the following year. Roosevelt was reelected in
his own right in 1904. He ran again for the presidency in 1912 on the
Progressive Party ticket, but was defeated.

ROSEWOOD One of a number of streets in Westwood Highlands whose
  Drive suffix is "wood."

ROSIE LEE Rosie Lee Williams was a prominent community leader in
Lane   Hunters Point during the 1960s when the Redevelopment
Authority's project there was under construction.

ROSS Merchant Charles L. Ross was an alderman in the early 1850s.
Alley

ROSSI Angelo Rossi was mayor of San Francisco for 14 years starting in
Avenue 1929. During his tenure, the Civic Center was completed and the
tax rate was reduced to its lowest level in 25 years.

ROUSSEAU Named for a Belgian friend of the De Boom family, the fa-
Street   ther of Charles and Oliver Rousseau of yachting fame. The
De Booms owned the tract of land on which this street is to be found.

RUCKMAN Named in 1923 to honor Major General John W. Ruckman,
Avenue   the commanding officer of Fort Baker from February 1909,
until November 1910.

RUSS Immanuel Charles Christian Russ arrived in San Francisco with
Street his family on March 26, 1847. Since he had been a jeweler in New
York, Russ opened a jewelry store upon his arrival. During the Gold Rush,
he operated an assay office. His family built a hotel on Montgomery Street
near the site of the Russ building. The purchase of the hotel land was for
less than $50.

RUSSIA Named after the country whose name is derived from the Rus, a
Avenue   nomadic tribe of Eastern Slavs who roamed the Upper Volga
River area in the ninth century.

RUSSIAN HILL See Russian Hill in the City Landmark section of this
Place   book.

RUTLAND Possibly named after the city in Vermont named for Rut-
Street   land, Massachusetts. In turn, this town was probably named
after either a town in England or the Earls and Dukes of Rutland—an
English title held by members of the Manners family from 1525.

SACRAMENTO Named after the capital of California situated in
Street   the Central Valley where the American and Sacramento rivers meet. This community was named for the Sacramento river. Originally called Rio de San Francisco, the name of the
river was changed to Spanish, for the Holy Sacrament. This was
originally a term in Roman law to describe a legal sanction, but now
has become a convenient expression for a sign or symbol of a sacred
thing, occasion, or event. Sacramento Street was originally called
Howard Street in honor of William Howard, a member of the first
City Council.

SAINT CHARLES Possibly named after the well-known street of the
Avenue   same name in New Orleans.

SAINT ELMO The name Saint Elmo is an Italian corruption of St. Eras-
Way   mus, the patron saint of Mediterranean sailors.

SAINT FRANCIS Named after Saint Francis of Assisi, for whom San
Boulevard   Francisco was named.

SAINT GERMAIN There are at least two important Saints Germain.
Avenue The first is Saint Germain of Auxerre (378–448), an important Gallic prelate twice sent on crucial missions from Rome to England to help consolidate the British church. Another is Saint Germain of Paris (496–576), an abbot and bishop, who was one of France's most revered saints and an important, though unsuccessful, mediator in the fratricidal civil war among several Merovingian Kings.

SAINT JOSEPH'S Named after Saint Joseph, the foster father of Christ
Avenue and husband of the Virgin Mary. This street received its name because it was situated next to the Catholic cemetery, Calvary.

SAINT LOUIS Probably named after Saint Louis (1274–1297), who was
Alley the great-nephew of Saint Louis, King of France. The former was confined in Barcelona for seven years as hostage for his father, a prisoner of war. Upon his release, Saint Louis joined the Franciscan order and was appointed Bishop of Toulouse.

SAINT MARY'S Named for St. Mary's College, once located nearby.
Avenue

SALINAS Named after the river and county seat which was named for
Avenue the salt marshes and ponds near the river mouth.

SALMON Named after the fish.
Street

SAMOSET Named after a 17th-century Pemaquid Indian who be-
Street friended the Pilgrims after they landed at Massachusetts.

SAN ANDREAS San Andreas was the name of an early ranch. San An-
Way dreas (or St. Andrew) was one of the Apostles and patron Saint of Scotland. He was the elder brother of St. Peter, and a disciple of St. John the Baptist. Tradition has it that he was crucified in Greece during the reign of Nero, in 60 A.D.

SAN ANSELMO San Anselmo was the name of an early large ranch. It
Avenue was situated in Marin County where the town and adjacent valley with the same name are to be found. The name of the ranch was probably first named for a local Indian with "San" added subsequently, or after St. Anselm (1033–1109).

SAN ANTONIO Probably named after Saint Anthony of Padua, patron
Place saint of the Franciscan Order. He joined the Order in 1221, and died at Padua in 1231. He was noted as a preacher and worker of miracles.

SAN BENITO Named for an early large ranch which in turn was named
Way for St. Benedict, founder of the Benedictine Order.

SAN BUENAVENTURA Named after the Mission which was founded
Way in Ventura, California, in 1782. The mission was named to honor St. Bonaventure, a Franciscan, in the thirteenth century.

SAN CARLOS Named after Mission San Carlos Borromeo, founded in
Street 1770 in Monterey. This mission was named to honor St. Charles Borromeo (1538–1584), Archbishop of Milan.

SAN DIEGO Named after Mission San Diego de Alcalá, founded in 1769
Avenue   in what is now San Diego. It was the first mission in California and it was named to honor San Diego de Alcalá, a Franciscan saint in the fifteenth century.

SAN FELIPE Named after an early large ranch which in turn was named
Avenue   after one of the several St. Phillips.

SAN FERNANDO Named after Mission San Fernando Rey de España,
Way   founded in 1797 in San Fernando, California. This mission was named to honor St. Ferdinand III, King of Leon and Castile.

SAN GABRIEL Named after Mission San Gabriel Archangel, founded
Avenue   in 1771 in San Gabriel, California, just east of Los Angeles. The mission was named to honor the Archangel Gabriel, "the angel of the Incarnation and of Consolation and of the Power of God."

SAN JACINTO Named after an early large ranch probably named after
Way   St. Hyacinth of Silesia.

SAN JOSE Named after the Mission San José which was founded near
Avenue   San José in 1797. In turn, this city was named for St. Joseph, the foster father of Christ.

SAN JUAN Named after the Mission San Juan Bautista which was
Avenue   founded in 1797 in the town of San Juan Bautista near Hollister. In English, the name of the mission means "St. John, the Baptist."

SAN LEANDRO Named after the early large ranch (1839) located in the
Way   vicinity of this East Bay community. It was probably named after St. Leander, Archbishop of Seville.

SAN LORENZO Named after the early large ranch which was named
Way   after St. Lawrence, possibly the third century St. Lawrence of Rome who was roasted to death by Emperor Valerian in 258 AD.

SAN LUIS Named after the Mission San Luis Obispo de Tolosa (Saint
Avenue   Louis, Bishop of Toulouse) which was established in 1772 by Junípero Serra. Saint Louis (1274–1297) was the great nephew of St. Louis, King of France.

SAN MARCOS Saint Mark, the Evangelist, is the traditional author of the
Avenue   second Gospel of the New Testament. Along with Peter and Paul, he is considered to be a first-generation Apostle.

SAN MATEO Named after the Mission hospice which was built in this
Avenue   West Bay community in 1793. This name was derived from a nearby dry river bed named by Anza in 1776 to honor St. Matthew, the evangelist, apostle, and legendary author of one of the four Gospels.

SAN MIGUEL San Miguel, an early Mexican land grant, occupied the area
Street   in which this street is situated. This ranch may have been named after Mission San Miguel Archangel which was founded in 1797 in San Miguel. The mission and town were named for Archangel Michael.

SAN PABLO Named after the early large ranch which was named for
Avenue   St. Paul the Apostle.

SAN RAFAEL Named after the Mission San Rafael Archangel, founded
Way   in San Rafael, now the county seat of Marin, in 1817.
St. Rafael the Archangel was one of three angels venerated by the Catholic Church.

SAN RAMON Named after the early large ranch which was probably
Way   named for St. Raymond, a Roman martyr.

SANCHEZ José Antonio Sánchez, a son of one of Anza's soldiers and a
Street   famous Indian fighter, was a commander of the Presidio. His
family acquired extensive land holdings south of present-day South San
Francisco. Sánchez is buried in the cemetery at Mission Dolores.

SANSOME Named after a street of the same name in downtown Phila-
Street   delphia by Jean Jacques Vioget, a Swiss sailor, surveyor, and
the city's first municipal engineer. There is also reason to suspect that
George Hyde, a city official (but a native of Philadelphia) also proposed
this street's name in 1847. Philadelphia's Sansom Street (without the "e")
was named for William Sansom, a home-builder who conceived the concept of row houses in 1803.

SANTA ANA Named after an early large ranch which in turn was named
Avenue   after St. Anne, the mother of the Virgin Mary.

SANTA BARBARA Named after the mission established in 1786. The
Avenue   city was named to honor the patron saint of mariners by Sebastian Vizcaíno in 1602.

SANTA CLARA Named after the Mission Santa Clara de Asís which was
Avenue   founded in Santa Clara in 1777. Saint Clare of As-
sísi was co-founder of the Franciscan order of Poor Charles. She was the
first woman to embrace the Franciscan order in the 13th century.

SANTA CRUZ Named after the mission which was established in Santa
Avenue   Cruz in 1791. This is the Spanish for "Holy Cross."

SANTA MONICA Named for an early large ranch. Saint Monica was the
Way   mother of Saint Augustine.

SANTA PAULA Named after an early large ranch. Saint Paula was a
Avenue   noble Roman matron who became a disciple of Saint
Jerome.

SANTA RITA Named after an early large ranch. Saint Rita de Casis was
Avenue   an Augustinian.

SANTA YNEZ Named after Santa Ines Mission which was founded in
Avenue   1804 in Solvang. Saint Ines was named to honor Saint
Agnes of Assisi who lived in the 13th century. She was a sister of St. Clare
and one of the first to embrace the religious life under the rule of St.
Francis as a Poor Clare or Minoress.

SANTA YSABEL Named after an early large ranch which was probably
Avenue   named in honor of Saint Elizabeth of Portugal, daughter of the King of Aragon.

SANTIAGO Named by the Parkside Realty Company, the developers of
Street   this area around the turn of the century. It was probably

named for the *Santiago*, a sailing ship which visited San Diego and Monterey hauling provisions and personnel for Anza's expedition of 1776.

SANTOS
Street In Portuguese, this means "saints."

SATURN
Street Named after the god of sowing or seed in Roman mythology.

SAWYER
Street Henry Schwerin, the developer of Visitacion Valley Homestead, named this street after a friend in 1868.

SCENIC
Way An appropriate name for a street that has a beautiful view of the Golden Gate.

SCHWERIN
Street Henry Schwerin, a native of Germany, arrived in San Francisco about January, 1850. One year later he established a bakery business and after marrying Ottilia – for whom a street is named in Daly City – he moved to a 300 acre parcel in Visitacion Valley which he subdivided in April, 1868. His son, Ted, married Kate McCarthy whose father, Peter is reputed also to have been the namesake of a street in the area.

SCOTIA
Avenue The name originated in the 11th century when *Scotia* was given to the southwestern tract of what is now Scotland. This land was settled by a tribe of Scots who had migrated from Ireland.

SCOTLAND
Avenue Named after the country which was originally known as Caledonia. The name originated from a group of Scots who had migrated to this area in the eleventh century.

SCOTT
Street General Winfield Scott, a U.S. General in three wars, was the unsuccessful Whig candidate for President in 1852. Scott commanded the U.S. Army at the outbreak of the Civil War as well as participating in the War of 1812 and in the Mexican War. A post within the Presidio is also named for him. He also has the distinction of being one of only three individuals with both their first and last names on two different streets. The other street is Winfield Street and the other persons are Mark Aldrich and Fernando Rivera y Moncada.

SEA CLIFF
Avenue Named for the district which in turn derives its name from the physical geography of the area.

SEA VIEW
Terrace As the name implies, there is a good view of the ocean from this street.

SEAL ROCK
Drive Named for seal rock where the sea lions live and play.

SECURITY PACIFIC
Place This alley was formerly Savings Union Place. The name was changed because a different bank occupied space along this thoroughfare.

SELBY
Street Thomas H. Selby, a New York merchant, came to San Francisco hoping to earn enough to pay his creditors after his eastern business had failed in 1849. He was successful as a metal importer, and in 1851 was elected a member of the Board of Aldermen where he led an effort to reorganize the Police Department. In 1869, he was elected to a four-year term as mayor by only 110 votes. Selby also founded the Selby Smelting Company and built the Selby Shot Tower.

SEMINOLE Named after the Iroquois-speaking tribe that lived in what is
  Avenue now western New York State and eastern Ohio. They were
the largest and one of the most important of the original five nations of the
Iroquois League. Names were given between 1863 and 1865 to a number of
streets in the south central part of the city after Indian tribes of New York
State.

SENECA Named after the Iroquois-speaking tribe that lived in what is
  Avenue now western New York State and eastern Ohio. They were the
largest and one of the most important of the original five nations of the
Iroquois League.

SERRANO Doña Ana Regina Serrano is the origin of this street name.
  Drive

SEVILLE Named after the city in southern Spain, important in history as
  Street a cultural center, a capital of Muslim Spain, and a center for
Spanish exploration of the New World.

SEWARD Probably named for the Secretary of State under both Abra-
  Street ham Lincoln and Andrew Johnson who conducted the nego-
tiations with Russia to purchase Alaska in 1867. For a time, Alaska was
known as "Seward's Folly," since the price was outrageous at that time,
7.2 million dollars.

SHAFTER (Also Road) Named in 1939 to honor General William R.
  Avenue Shafter, commander of the United States Army in Cuba.
General Shafter received the Medal of Honor for his bravery in the Civil
War. He also was commanding officer of the Department of California
from May 1877 to 1898 and again from 1899 to 1901.

SHAKESPEARE Named after the British playwright and poet, widely
  Street regarded as the greatest writer of all time. His plays,
written in the late 16th and early 17th centuries for a small repertory
theatre, are today performed more often and in more countries than ever
before. As Ben Jonson said, "Shakespeare was not of an age, but for all
time."

SHARON Lawyer William Sharon came west from Mississippi in 1849.
  Street He was a realtor, banker, miner, and United States Senator.
Despite the fact that his donation was instrumental in building Golden
Gate Park's Children's Playground—the first of its kind in the United
States—Sharon was a crafty and sometimes shady manipulator of men
and money.

SHAWNEE Named after the Algonquian-speaking North American In-
  Avenue dian tribe whose first known home was the central Ohio
River Valley. They now reside in Oklahoma.

SHELLEY John F. Shelley, the thirty-fifth mayor of San Francisco
  Drive (1964–1968) was born in the South Park district in 1905. At
thirty-two, he became president of the San Francisco Labor Council. He
was a Congressman prior to assuming the city's highest office and experi-
enced a turbulent term, prompting one observer to note that he was the
city's "unluckiest Mayor."

SHERMAN (Also Road) Lt. General William Tecumseh Sherman was an
Street   American Civil War General now considered an important
theoretician of modern warfare. Prior to his participation in the Civil War,
Sherman ran the Bank of Lucas Turner in San Francisco. Sherman led the
Union forces in crushing campaigns through the South. He is often quoted
as saying "War is Hell."

SHERWOOD Located half a block from Robin Hood Drive, this street
Court   may have been named for Sherwood Forest, a haunt of this
legendary outlaw. In addition, most of the streets in Westwood Highlands
have the suffix "wood."

SHORE VIEW A view of the south shore of Marin County may be
Terrace   obtained from this street.

SHORT By no means the shortest street in San Francisco, the name may
Street   be derived from the fact that this thoroughfare is only one block
long.

SHOTWELL J. M. Shotwell was the secretary of the Merchant's Ex-
Street   change and a cashier in Alsop and Company's bank.

SHRADER A. I. Shrader, a member of the Board of Supervisors from the
Street   Ninth Ward from 1865 to 1872, was instrumental in the creation of Golden Gate Park.

SIERRA Named for the California county which was named after the
Street   Spanish word for "saw-tooth mountain range." Sierra Nevada
means the "snowy mountain range" or the "sierra white as snow," while
the Sierra Madre is the "Mother Sierra," so called because it was thought
at first that the other outstanding mountain ranges of North America
emanated from this chain.

SILVER Named for a pioneer family which had large property interests
Avenue   in San Francisco and Monterey Counties.

SIMONDS Named in honor of Major General George S. Simonds in 1940.
Loop   Simonds was Acting Chief of Staff from 1927 until 1931, and
Deputy Chief of Staff from 1935 to 1936. He died at Letterman General
Hospital in the Presidio.

SKYLINE Although a view of San Francisco's skyline is not forthcoming
Boulevard   from this thoroughfare, an excellent panorama of San Francisco's mountain range (Twin Peaks, Mt. Davidson, and Mt. Sutro) can be
seen from the southern part.

SKYVIEW Most of the streets in this residential subdivision, nestled
Way   near the top of Twin Peaks, have "view" for a suffix.

SLOAT Commodore John Drake Sloat took command of the U.S. Navy
Boulevard   squadron in the Pacific in 1846. Sloat captured Monterey on
July 7th of that year, and two days later, on orders, Montgomery landed
and seized Yerba Buena, the village that would soon be San Francisco,
from the Mexicans.

SOLA Don Pablo Vicente de Sola was the tenth governor of California
Avenue   (1815–1823), the last under Spanish rule. Sola was originally a
soldier who came with Anza when he established a settlement in 1776.

SOMERSET Probably named after the town in southwestern England.
Street

SONOMA Probably named after the county which lies north of San Fran-
Street cisco and Marin. In turn, this county was named either for an
Indian word meaning "valley of the moon" or for the Patwin Indian word
for "nose," the reference being to the land or tribe of "Chief Nose."

SOTELO Named for a member of the Anza expedition who was one of
Avenue the first settlers in San Francisco.

SOUTH HILL This street goes up (and down) South Hill which origi-
Boulevard nally got its name because of its location in the southern
portion of San Francisco.

SOUTH PARK South Park was created in 1854 by Englishman George
Avenue Gordon in an attempt to recreate a residential block of
London. For several years, it was a very stylish address. The street runs
parallel to, and takes its name from, the park located south of the prevailing
center of town.

SOUTH VAN NESS Originally for most of its length this street was an
Avenue extension of Howard Street, but Howard Street had
an unsavory reputation so the residents of this part did not want to be
associated with this name and so they opted for the present one. For its
origin see Van Ness Avenue.

SOUTHERN HEIGHTS The name of this street stems from its location
Avenue on the slope of Potrero Hill; at the time of its
creation, this street was situated in the southern part of town.

SOUTHWOOD The southernmost of all the streets in Westwood Park.
Drive All the thoroughfares have the same suffix "wood."

SPARROW Named a number of years ago by the neighborhood boys for
Street their nemesis – "Old Man Sparrow."

SPARTA Named after the Greek town famed for its military oligarchy.
Street Sparta emerged as the most powerful state in Greece, defeat-
ing Athens in the Peloponnesian War of 404 B.C.

SPEAR This street was probably named for Nathan Spear, an immigrant
Street to California in 1832. Four years later, he moved to Yerba Buena
where he and two partners operated a store and trading post. He helped
erect the first frame house in San Francisco in 1836. Three years later, he
built the first flour mill in California. Although less likely, it is also possible
that this street might have been named after Forty-Niner Willis Bradford
Spear, an army scout with General Winfield Scott in Mexico. He bought
the first lot—underwater at the time—on what is now Spear Street.

SPRINGFIELD Possibly named after the town in Massachusetts (or Illi-
Drive nois or Ohio or New Jersey or Vermont), all of which
were named after a town in England. There are only a handful of states
which do not have a town called Springfield; Pennsylvania has two of them.

SPROUL This street was formerly Yerba Buena Lane. Starting to work
Lane for the Southern Pacific Railroad in 1882, William Sproul rose
through the ranks to become its President in 1911. He built a large mansion

at the intersection of Yerba Buena with Sacramento Street. After his death, his widow prevailed upon the city to have the name of the street changed in his honor.

STANFORD   Leland Stanford (1824–1893) started as a grocer and be-
Street   came governor of California, a member of the United States Senate, a railroad builder, and founder of one of the greatest universities in America. He was a member of the "Big Four"—owners of the Central Pacific railroad which became part of the Southern Pacific railroad which recently merged with the Santa Fe railroad.

STANFORD HEIGHTS   See above.
Avenue

STANLEY   Ira Stanley was a Forty-Niner.
Street

STANTON   Perhaps the last street in the city to remain unpaved. Who
Street   the street was named for is unknown.

STANYAN   (Also Boulevard) C. H. Stanyan was a supervisor and a mem-
Street   ber of the Commission to Appraise Outside Lands in 1872. This meant everything west of Divisadero Street. Stanyan fought unsuccessfully to have the Golden Gate Park Panhandle extended as a parkway all the way to Market Street.

STARR KING   Rev. Thomas Starr King, born in New York in 1824, was
Way   spiritual leader of San Francisco's First Unitarian Church. At twenty-one, he was ordained in the ministry; two years later he was asked to come to San Francisco. He soon began making passionate pro-Union speeches in what is now Union Square. He died at age forty. His sarcophagus may be found in the churchyard of the First Unitarian Church adjacent to this street.

STARVIEW   One of a number of streets in this residential subdivision
Way   which have "view" for their suffix.

STEINER   L. Steiner was a good friend of Charles Gough, a member of a
Street   committee to lay out and name streets in the Western Addition in 1855. Steiner delivered water in the area in 1850.

STEUART   William M. Steuart came to California aboard the United
Street   States battleship *Ohio* in 1849. He was a member of the town council in 1849–50 and a delegate to, and acting chairman of, the California State Constitutional Convention at Monterey in 1849. This Constitution not only guaranteed the right to pursue happiness but also to obtain it. Soon thereafter, Steuart was an unsuccessful candidate for governor.

STEVENSON   Colonel Jonathan Drake Stevenson, an officer of the First
Street   New York Volunteers, arrived in California in March, 1847, to fight in the Mexican War. Resigning from the Army a year later, Stevenson turned to mining gold. He later bought real estate in Santa Cruz and San Francisco.

STILWELL   Probably named after "Vinegar Joe" or "Uncle Joe" Stil-
Road   well, the World War II army officer who headed both the United States and Chinese nationalist resistance to the Japanese advance

on the Chinese mainland. After the war, Stilwell served as Sixth Army Commander until his death at the Presidio—the location of this street.

STOCKTON Commodore Robert F. Stockton arrived in Monterey in
Street   command of the U.S.S. *Congress* eight days after Sloat took California for the United States. He was appointed military governor of California, holding the post for the first six months of American jurisdiction. Stockton's grandfather was a member of the Continental Congress, and the city of Stockton was named for him by Captain Charles M. Weber.

STONECREST A handsome name for a street in the Lakeside subdivision
Drive   whose origin was inspired by the name of the developers, Henry and Bill Stoneson.

STONEMAN Possibly named after George Stoneman (1822–94) who
Street   was born in New York. He came to California in 1846 as a lieutenant in the Mormon battalion, served with the Pacific railroad survey in 1853, and with the Union army as a General during the Civil War. He participated in the engagement at Chancellorsville and freed the Union prisoners at Andersonville. After the war, Stoneman returned to California where he was governor from 1883 to 1887.

STONEYBROOK A handsome name for a street in the Lakeside subdivi-
Avenue   sion whose origin was inspired by the name of the developers, Henry and Bill Stoneson.

STONEYFORD See the above street name explanation.
Avenue

STORRIE Named for the street's builder, contractor Robert Storrie. It
Street   was built with leftover right-of-way from the Twin Peaks tunnel in 1918.

STRATFORD Probably named after Shakespeare's birthplace in En-
Drive   gland. It stands where a Roman road crossed the river.

SUMMIT This street sits atop one of the many hills in San Francisco.
Street   The number of hills depends upon what one considers to be a hill; however, most experts agree that the number varies between 10 and 42.

SUNRISE More of a hope than a promise. The sunrise is visible from this
Way   street, if one is awake at the appropriate hour.

SUNSET Not named after the famous thoroughfare of the same name in
Boulevard Hollywood and Los Angeles, but after the district in this city through which this street passes. The neighborhood is in the extreme western part of San Francisco, where the sun sets into the Pacific Ocean.

SUNVIEW A view of the sun and the City below may be obtained from
Drive   this street near the top of the main approach to Twin Peaks.

SURREY Probably named after the county in southeastern England ad-
Street   joining the River Thames. Its name means "southern district" in the Saxon language.

SUSSEX Named after one of the kingdoms of Anglo-Saxon England now
Street known as the county of Sussex. This name is derived from the
Old English *Suo Seax* (South Saxons.)

SUTRO HEIGHTS Adolph Sutro, twenty-first mayor of San Francisco
Avenue (1895–97), started as a cigar dealer. Self-educated,
Sutro became a noted mining engineer, winning fame and fortune by driv-
ing a five-mile tunnel into the Comstock Lode in Nevada. Several other
landmarks are named for him, not the least of which is Mount Sutro. A
great civic benefactor, Sutro sponsored tree-plantings throughout the city.

SUTTER John A. Sutter, a Swiss adventurer, arrived in Yerba Buena in
Street 1839. The Mexican government granted him large holdings of
land in the Sacramento Valley where he raised crops. In January, 1848 a
carpenter named James Wilson Marshall found a few flakes of gold while
building a sawmill for Sutter on the south fork of the American River at
Colma. Marshall brought the gold to Sutter at the place now known as
Sutter's Fort. The news soon leaked out—the Gold Rush began. Curiously,
however, both Sutter and Marshall ended their lives in poverty.

SWEENY Surveyor John Sweeny was employed by the Crocker Build-
Street ing and Land Company in the 1880s during the subdivision of
the Crocker estate. The estate was located where the street is to be found.

SWISS Probably named after the adjective pertaining to Switzerland, the
Avenue native country of one of the pioneers. These two words – Swiss
and Switzerland – are derived from Schwyz, one of the original cantons or
districts of this country which, along with two other districts, formed the
nucleus of this nation in the thirteenth century.

SYLVAN This street bisects Eucalyptus, is located two blocks west of
Drive Forest View, and is derived from the Latin word for forest;
however that is its only association with trees.

TACOMA Named after the Indian name for Mt. Rainier, Washing-
Street ton's highest mountain.

TAMALPAIS Tamalpais is a Miwok Indian word, probably meaning
Terrace "bay mountain." Since, however, the southern coast
Miwok Indians were called "Tamales" by the Spaniards, it seems more
likely that it was the name of a village of the Tamal Indians at the foot of
the mountain and meant "the Tamales by the mountain." (See also Mount
Tamalpais in the Bay Area Landmarks section).

TANDANG SORA Tandang Sora was a hero in the Philippine struggle
Street against the Spanish in the 1890s. In 1979 the street
name was changed from O'Doul Lane commemorating the San Francisco
baseball hero who was originally a pitcher, then an outfielder, and finally, a
manager of the beloved home town Seals for seventeen seasons.

TAPIA Felipe Santiago Tapia was a soldier and settler in San Jose be-
Drive tween 1786 and 1790. Born in 1745 in Culiacan, he was chosen as
a recruit for Anza's party of 1776. He brought with him his wife and nine
children. They baptized five more children in Santa Clara between 1778
and 1786.

TARA Between the 1st and 4th centuries, Tara was the seat of the ruling
Street   clan of County Mead, Ireland.

TARAVAL Named for Anza's Indian guide in 1776.
Street

TAYLOR (Also Road) Named after General Zachary Taylor (1784-1850),
Street   the hero of Buena Vista and twelfth president of the United
States. Taylor's nickname was "old rough and ready." His term in office
was cut short by an untimely death.

TEHAMA There are three theories as to the origin of this name. Tehama
Street   is said to have been derived from the Mexican word for
"shingle." A more likely theory is that the word is of Indian origin and,
perhaps, may mean "high water." The Tehama Indian Tribe resided in
what is now the northern portion of the Sacramento valley. The most likely
explanation is that this street was made quite famous in the 1890s because
many chorus girls who worked in the Old Tivoli Opera House on Eddy
Street lived along it. To compete with the wealthy women from Nob Hill
who were bedecked with diamonds and sealskin coats these girls wore an
imitation sealskin which was made from dog skins and cat fur. It was called
"Tehama Sealskin."

TELEGRAPH HILL (Also Place) This street received its name from the
Boulevard   fact that it goes to (and from) and is adjacent to
Telegraph Hill. (See Telegraph Hill in the Landmark section of this book.)

TEMESCAL This is an Indian word of Aztec origin which means "seat
Terrace   house." A temescal was an Indian sauna, a low dugout
covered with rocks.

TEMPLE This street bisects Saturn Street. Saturn's temple still stands
Street   (in part) in Rome: therefore, this street may have been given
this name to commemorate Saturn's temple.

TENNESSEE Named after the state and the river whose name came
Street   from an important Cherokee town located on the Little
Tennessee River and spelled variously *Tanase, Tennassee, Tanasi,* or
Tinasse. The meaning of the name is unknown.

TERRA VISTA The name combines the Latin *terra*, meaning "land"
Avenue   with the Spanish *vista*, meaning "view."

TEXAS Named after the state whose name comes from an Indian varia-
Street   tion, *texia,* of Spanish *tejas,* "allies," used by various tribes in
reference to their mutually protective alliances.

THOMAS General George H. Thomas was the commanding general of
Avenue   the Division of the Pacific from 1869 to 1870. Known as "the
Rock of Chickamauga," Thomas participated in both the Florida and Civil
Wars. He died in San Francisco.

THOMAS MORE Named for the Church of the same name which is situ-
Way   ated on this thoroughfare. Thomas More (1477–1535),
the British humanist and statesman, was put to death for refusing to ac-
cept King Henry VIII as head of the Church of England.

THOR   Named after the deity common to all early Germanic peoples.
Avenue   Thor, a great warrior, was represented as a red-bearded, middle-aged man of enormous strength, an implacable foe of Giants but benevolent toward mankind.

TIFFANY   Robert J. Tiffany's story was typical of many pioneers. A native of New York, he left for California in 1849 when news of
Avenue
the gold discoveries reached him. He arrived in San Francisco on July 9, 1850, after a boat trip which went around Cape Horn. Tiffany was an unlucky gold miner and eventually returned to New York. Returning in 1853, he opened a hat store which flourished. Tiffany bought land and became head of the People's Homestead, a property development firm, as well as a bank director and president of the Association of California Pioneers in 1866.

TILLMAN   Named after the Tillman family of safe builders who lived on
Place   this little alley.

TIOGA   In the Iroquois, *tioga* means "where it forks." The name was
Avenue   given to an Iroquois village in central Pennsylvania located
where the Susquehanna joins with the Chemung river. It is also the name of a county in New York, probably the direct origin of this street name.

TOCOLAMA   The word *tokoloma* exists in the central Sierra Miwok
Avenue   Indian Language and means "land salamander." The street
was named for the town in Marin County.

TOLAND   (Also Place) Doctor Hugh Huga Toland was a noted surgeon
Street   (1806–1880) who pioneered corrective surgery for club feet.
Toland reached San Francisco in 1853 and was called "the great surgeon of the Pacific Coast." He founded Toland Medical College in San Francisco, turned over to the University of California in 1873.

TOLEDO   Named after the city in south central Spain. In 193 B.C., To-
Way   ledo was captured by the Romans. As Toletum, it became an
important Roman colony. The present name evolved from the Latin.

TOPEKA   After the capital city of Kansas whose name is of uncertain In-
Avenue   dian origin. One interpretation is "smoky hill," while another is
"a good place to dig potatoes." It is said that the Indian term refers to any edible root, not specifically potato.

TOVAR   Don Pedro Tovar was an officer in Coronado's army.
Avenue

TOWNSEND   Doctor James Townsend came overland to California in
Street   1844. Under Governor Richard B. Mason, Townsend was
president of the town council and one of the leading citizens in San Francisco between 1845 and 1850.

TOYON   This is the name of a beautiful shrub, also known as Christmas
Lane   berry and California holly.

TRADER VIC   Formerly Agate Alley. The name was changed in 1985 to
Alley   honor Vic Bergeron (1902-1984). He opened the first
Trader Vic restaurant in 1934, across the Bay in Emeryville. As of this

writing (1986) there are 22 such restaurants including the one that is at the end of this alley.

TRANSVERSE This road cuts across and runs through Golden Gate
Drive Park. A similarly named drive crosses Central Park in New York City.

TREAT George Treat was an early settler who owned famous race
Avenue horses. In his later years, Treat became interested in Mexican mining ventures.

TRENTON Probably named after the capital city of New Jersey. In 1714
Street William Trent, a Philadelphia merchant, bought 800 acres and laid out the town which was named in his honor in 1721.

TRINITY Named after the Holy Trinity.
Street

TULANE Named after the university in New Orleans. In the late 1860s
Avenue many of the streets in this part of town were named after colleges and universities by the land developers—the University Homestead Association.

TUNNEL This road runs adjacent to the Southern Pacific railroad
Avenue tracks. At the street's end, these tracks enter a tunnel which burrows under one of San Francisco's nameless southern hills.

TURK Lawyer Frank Turk came to San Francisco in 1849 and worked in
Street the post office for John W. Geary. At the first election of local officers in that same year, Turk was elected second *alcalde* (magistrate). He later became a clerk of the town council. At one time, Turk owned nearly all of what is now known as Nob Hill.

TUSCANY Named after the district in west central Italy. The name Tus-
Alley cany is derived from an Etruscan tribe who settled there around 1000 B.C. *Tuscia* came into official use under the Roman empire in the third century A.D.

TWIN PEAKS See Twin Peaks in the City Landmarks section of this
Boulevard book.

UGARTE During the late seventeenth century John Ugarte
Street founded missions in Lower California.

ULLOA Francisco de Ulloa was a navigator and a member of the Portolá
Street expedition to Northern California. The street was named by the developers of this area, the Parkside Realty Company, around the turn of the century.

UNDERWOOD Named for General Franklin Underwood.
Avenue

UNION The origin of this name is unknown. It appears on William
Street Eddy's survey of 1849 and may refer to the Union of States which California joined but this is uncertain. Union Square did not receive its name until several years later.

UNIVERSITY Named for and by the University Homestead Associ-
Avenue ation which developed this area in the late 1860s. In turn,

this name originated from the fact that an academy, the University Mound College, was situated nearby. This institution started as a boys' high school in 1859.

UPPER Terrace One of two streets—the other is Lower Terrace—on the slope of Mount Olympus.

UPTON Street Probably named for Matthias Gilbert Upton, the principal editor and writer on the *Alta California*, one of San Francisco's first newspapers, and a political and commercial force in California.

URANUS Terrace Named after the personification of Heaven in Greek mythology. There is also, of course, the planet Uranus, and this street runs into another such street—Saturn. These streets are situated on the slopes of Mt. Olympus.

URBANO Drive This street is in the form of an oval, and was once a race track for horses. The origin of the name, however, is unknown.

UTAH Street Named after the state whose name is derived from the Indian name *Ute* or *Eutaw,* an Indian tribe who inhabited this area for more than a century. The word has been variously defined to mean: "in the tops of the mountains," "high-up," "the land of the sun," and "the land of plenty."

VALENCIA Street Named either for José Manuel Valencia, a soldier in Anza's company, or for his son, Candelario Valencia, in the military service at the Presidio and later a ranch owner near Lafayette in Contra Costa County. He also owned property adjoining the Mission Dolores, located two blocks from this street.

VALLEJO Street General Mariano Guadalupe Vallejo, the most important and respected Mexican citizen during the American settlement and seizure of California, was commander of the Presidio in San Francisco in 1835. Later, General Vallejo remained active in the State's affairs and served as a member of California's Constitutional Convention of 1849. It was at Vallejo's Sonoma estate that California's short-lived "Bear Flag Republic" was proclaimed.

VALLEY Street Although not quite in a valley, this east-west street goes across Noe Valley.

VALPARISO Street From the Portuguese for "valley of paradise." There is also a city with this name in Chile which was named after a city in Spain. San Francisco's second surveyor Jasper O'Farrell lived in this Chilean seaport in the 1840s before moving to San Francisco. Hence the selection of this particular name.

VAN BUREN Street Probably named after Martin Van Buren (1782–1862), eighth president of the United States, one of the founders of the Democratic Party. Van Buren, known as the "Little Magician," was a skillful and cunning politician.

VAN DYKE Avenue Lawyer Walter Van Dyke, a native of New York, came overland to California soon after the discovery of gold. The first elected district attorney of Trinity County, he was appointed United States District Attorney in 1873. Later, he became a justice of the Supreme Court of California.

VAN NESS The widest street (125 feet) in San Francisco was named for
Avenue James Van Ness, the mayor of San Francisco in 1856. In
1855, he authored the ordinance granting Western Addition land titles to
those who actually possessed the property. Van Ness served as an alderman before being elected mayor; afterwards he became a farmer in San
Luis Obispo. He ended his political career as a state senator in 1871.

VARELA Casimiro Varela holds the dual distinction of being one of the
Avenue first settlers of both San Francisco (1777) and Los Angeles
(1790). Varela and his wife came with Anza. Their daughter, Marta, was
baptized in 1778.

VEGA A common Spanish surname.
Street

VENTURA Named after a foreshortened version of San Buenaventura,
Avenue the leader of the Franciscan order after Saint Francis.

VENUS In Roman mythology, a goddess of agriculture. Her name, how-
Street ever, became associated with beauty, charm, and the power
of love.

VERMONT The second most crooked street in San Francisco with five
Street full and two half turns in the block between McKinley and
22nd Streets on Potrero Hill, the name comes from the state which in turn
received its name from the French *mont vert* or "green mountains."

VERONA Probably named after the province and city in northern Italy.
Place Founded by an ancient tribe, it became a Roman colony in
89 B.C. and rapidly rose in importance because of its strategic location
between Italy and northern Europe.

VESTA Named after the beautiful Roman goddess of the hearth, her
Street symbol. Her name is derived from a Sanskrit root *vas*, which
expresses the idea of "shining." Vesta also personified fire when used for
domestic or religious ceremonies.

VICENTE Probably named for a member of Anza's expedition to San
Street Francisco in 1776.

VICKSBURG Named after the Civil War Battle of Vicksburg which took
Street place near this city in Mississippi. In turn, the city was
named to honor Rev. Newitt Vick, a Methodist minister.

VICTORIA Probably named either after the British Queen (1819–1901)
Street whose long reign restored dignity and popularity to the British crown, possibly saving the monarchy from abolition, or for the ancient
Roman goddess of victory. Responsible for success in arms, she also pro-
tected fields and woods. Or possibly named for Manuel Victoria, governor
of this area in the Mexican period.

VIDAL Don Mariano Vidal was a purveyor for and a member of the Anza
Drive expedition to Northern California in 1776.

VIENNA Named after the capital of Austria whose name as Wenia
Street appeared for the first time in the Salzburg Annals in 881 A.D.

VILLA Originally a Roman term for a country estate complete with
Terrace house, grounds and subsidiary buildings, the word now refers to
a sumptuous suburban or country estate. Approximately two dozen
houses, or villas, if you will, share a superb view of the city from this street
which is terraced onto Twin Peaks.

VIRGIL Named for the great Roman poet, Virgil (70–19 B.C.), best
Street known for his epic, the *Aeneid*. This street is one block away
from Horace Street.

VIRGINIA After the girl's name or after the state which was named for
Street Elizabeth I, the "virgin queen."

VISITACION The name was originally given for the visitation of the
Avenue Virgin Mary to Saint Elizabeth. Visitacion Valley was a
tract of land granted to Jacob P. Leese in 1839 on which he was authorized
to build houses. The street runs through and its name is derived from this
area, located in the southern part of San Francisco.

VISTA This word means "view" in Italian, but in any language there is
Court not much of one from this residential street in the Presidio.

VISTA VERDE In Italian, this means "green view;" however, this name
Court was probably selected for its sound rather than its
meaning.

WABASH Probably named for the town and river in Indiana. The
Terrace name is derived from an Indian word meaning "shining
white" or "water over white stones."

WALLACE William T. Wallace was Chief Justice of the Supreme Court
Avenue of California elected in 1869. A Kentuckian who came west
in 1852, Wallace first practiced law in San Jose and became district attorney of Santa Clara County.

WALLEN Brigadier General Henry D. Wallen fought in both the Florida
Court and Civil Wars and was the commanding officer of the Presidio in late 1865 and early 1866.

WALLER R.H. Waller, the City Recorder in the 1850s, was an early man-
Street ager of the San Francisco Protestant Orphan Asylum located
on nearby Haight Street from 1853 until shortly after the earthquake of
1906 when it was razed.

WALTER U. LUM Walter Uriah Lum founded the Chinese Times, a
Place popular newspaper. In 1904 Lum created the Chinese
American citizens alliance which fought for the repeal of the Chinese Exclu-
sion Act, a discriminatory immigration law for Asians. Lum died in 1961 and
twenty-four years later this street which had been Brenham Place was
renamed for him. He became the first Chinese person to be so honored.

WALTHAM Possibly named after the city in Massachusetts which was
Street named for a town of the same name near London, England.

WASHINGTON (Also Boulevard) First United States President George
Street Washington was a Revolutionary War General and
"Father of His Country." Along with Montgomery, Kearny, and Clay – the

names of other streets – Washington has been in continuous usage as a street name longer than any other.

WATERLOO Named for the village in Belgium, the site of the battle
Street between Napoleon and the Duke of Wellington. Napoleon Street is nearby.

WAVERLY The name is probably taken from the title of Sir Walter
Place Scott's novel. There is also a street in New York with the same name. Originally, it was called Pike Street and was the location of "homes of ill repute." In the 1860s, the name was changed; the street remained just as notorious.

WAWONA According to some authorities, this is an Indian name which
Street means "big tree." It was selected by the Parkside Realty Company around the turn of the century.

WEBSTER Named either for Daniel Webster (1782-1852), an orator,
Street politician and lawyer, who brought cases before the United States Supreme Court and served as a Congressman, Senator, and Secretary of State, or for Noah Webster (1758-1843), the lexicographer, who is best known for his *American Spelling Book* (1783) and his *American Dictionary of the English Language* (1828).

WELSH Captain Charles Welsh was born in 1810 and arrived in San
Street Francisco on June 18, 1847. He built the first brick house in North Beach and died in 1883.

WEST GATE You won't find a west gate at this western entrance to
Drive Mount Davidson Manor, but in the 1920s, when this subdivision was built, this name suggested exclusivity and security.

WEST POINT This street is situated on the approach to Hunters Point,
Road just west of Middle Point Road.

WEST PORTAL This word is derived from the Latin word for gate. This
Avenue street is the western approach to the tunnel under Twin Peaks for the Muni Metro subway system running all the way under Market Street. There is no eastern entrance now, although there once was at Castro Street before the Market Street subway was built.

WEST VIEW Regretably, there is no view from this street. Indeed, on
Avenue the west are a series of houses fronting Cambridge Street. Whatever the original reason may have been for naming this street, it is certainly no longer applicable.

WESTBROOK Elouise Westbrook was a prominent community leader
Court in the 1960s at Hunters Point when the Redevelopment Authority's project there was developed.

WESTERN SHORE An appropriate name for a street in a housing
Lane project sponsored by the International Longshoremen's Union. The *Western Shore* was a three-masted, full-rigged ship built in 1874. Four years later, however, this vessel was lost on Duxbury Reef while bound for San Francisco from Puget Sound with a cargo of coal. During her career, she held the record for the three fastest consecutive runs on record from Portland to Liverpool, making the voyage in only 97 days.

WESTWOOD This residential subdivision has streets named after the
Drive   points of the compass with the common suffix "wood."
This is the most westerly of these streets. The area was developed in 1916.

WHALESHIP Named after a type of vessel often found in Yerba Buena
Plaza   Cove, the present site of the Golden Gateway complex
where this plaza is located. Yankee whaleships plied the Pacific in great
numbers in the early decades of the 19th century, becoming common in the
1820s when the Japan grounds were discovered. These were fertile hunting areas for sperm whales. By the mid 1820s, the whaleships started to
put in at San Francisco's harbor for beef, vegetables, wood, water, and
other provisions.

WHIPPLE Major General Emile W. Whipple died of battle wounds at
Avenue   Chancellorsville on May 4, 1863.

WHITFIELD Geneva Whitfield was a prominent community leader in
Court   Hunters Point during the 1960s when the Redevelopment
Authoritiy's project was under construction.

WHITNEY YOUNG Whitney Young, a black civil rights leader, spear-
Circle   headed the drive for equal opportunity for Blacks
in the United States during his ten years (1961–71) as head of the National
Urban League.

WILDWOOD One of a series of streets in Westwood Highlands which
Way   have the common suffix "wood."

WILLIAMS Named after the college in Williamstown, Massachusetts.
Avenue   This is one of a number of area streets named after colleges
and universities. The names were selected by the land developers, the
University Homestead Association, around the turn of the century.

WINFIELD There are two possible versions for the origin of this street
Street   name. For the most probable see Scott Street. The other
theory has it that the street was named for the Winfield family who once
lived on this, one of the last brick streets, in San Francisco. Formerly this
street was called Chapultepic Street.

WINDSOR This is an alley on Telegraph Hill whose adjacent alley is
Place   Castle Alley. Windsor Castle is one of the principal residences of the British royal family.

WISCONSIN Named after the state. The name given to the river and to
Avenue   this frontier territory in 1836 was an anglicized version of a
French rendering of an Indian name which according to one version means
"our homeland" and in another version "the gathering of the waters" or "a
grassy place."

WOODHAVEN Located in Forest Knolls where the street names were
Court   conceived to evoke sylvan images.

WOODLAND This street ends next to Sutro Forest; presumably there
Avenue   were more trees around it when it was named.

WOODSIDE There are presently some woods on one side of this street at
Avenue   the Laguna Honda Home.

WOODWARD
Street
Named after the hotelkeeper, Robert B. Woodward. From 1866 to 1883, Woodward Gardens stood at Thirteenth and Mission Streets near the location of this street. This place was a precursor to Disneyland; a private pleasure resort with a public botanical garden, a playground, a skating area, a bandstand, a concert stage, an aquarium, an art gallery, a zoo, and a lake with boats for hire.

WORCESTER
Street
Probably named for the city in Massachusetts named after the city in England located in an area formerly known as Worcestershire. This name may have come from William Worcester, an English topographer who lived in the fifteenth century.

WRIGHT
Loop
(Also Road) Brigadier General George Wright was commander of the Department of the Pacific from 1862 to 1864, and commander of the District of California from 1864 to 1865. Wright drowned when the *Brother Jonathan* sank off the north coast on July 30, 1865.

YALE
Street
Named after the University named for Eli Yale, its founder, in 1701.

YERBA BUENA
Avenue and Road
In Spanish, this means "good herb." It was the original name for San Francisco from its establishment as a village in 1834 until 1847.

YORBA
Street
Antonio Yorba was a sergeant of the Catalan volunteers with the Portolá expedition in 1769.

YORK
Street
Probably named after New York City and State which were named for the city in England located in the scenic Vale of York. The adjacent street, Hampshire, was also named for a state named after an English district.

YORKE
Way
Father Peter C. Yorke was the moving force behind one of San Francisco's bitterest and most bloody labor conflicts: the teamster-waterfront strike of 1901. Then 37 years old Father Yorke led the battle against the powerful employers' organization, the police, and other city authorities, for protecting strike breakers. He turned public opinion in favor of the workers. In 1903, Yorke moved to Oakland, but returned in 1911 as pastor of St. Peter's Parish, a position he held until his death in 1925.

YOSEMITE
Avenue
Named after the valley, falls, and national park whose name was derived from *Oosoomate*, meaning "grizzly bear." The Yosemite Indians were called "grizzlies" by their enemies.

SERGEANT JOHN V. YOUNG
Street
Named to honor a police officer who was killed while on duty at the Ingleside police station in 1971. This station is located on this street situated in Balboa Park.

YUKON
Street
Named after the Alaskan river and territory in northwestern Canada. The Indian word means "the river" or "big river."

ZAMPA
Lane
This is an appropriate name for a street in a housing project sponsored by the International Longshoremen's Union. The *Zampa* was a three-masted schooner built in 1887 at Port Madison, Wash-

---

ington. On July 17, 1904, she went aground at Point Leadbetter near Oysterville but, cheating the Pacific graveyard of this, she got off again, reportedly being the only vessel to have such an experience. She sailed between Hawaii and the South Seas in her earlier years and, after 1921, between Grey's Harbor and Honolulu, finally being wrecked three miles north of Grey's Harbor on April 26, 1926.

ZOE Street This is the Greek word for "life." It is also a woman's name; this street may have been named for a relative or friend of a pioneer.

ZOO Street This is the main approach to the San Francisco Zoo. This word is a shortened version of zoological which in turn is derived from both the Latin and Greek words for animals.

WAVERLY PLACE

BAY AREA LANDMARKS

ALCATRAZ ISLAND   In 1775, Captain Juan Manuel de Ayala gave the name *Isla de Alcatraces* or in English, Pelican Island, to the island we now call Yerba Buena (or "good herb" in English) located adjacent to Treasure Island between San Francisco and Oakland. A subsequent map maker misapplied the name to the smaller, barren island in 1826. The now-famous prison, nicknamed "The Rock," held Indians, Confederates, and deserters while an Army prison from 1859 until 1934 when it became a civilian prison until 1963. Among the more notorious inmates were : Al Capone, who resided there from 1934 to 1939, Robert Stroud, better known as the "Birdman of Alcatraz" (1942–1959), and the only public enemy personally arrested by J. Edgar Hoover, Alvin Karpis, who also had the dubious distinction of being the longest resident with a 27–year stint from 1936 until 1963. The island is now a part of the Golden Gate National Recreation Area and one of the most popular attractions in the entire National Park system.

ANGEL ISLAND   Captain Juan Manuel de Ayala anchored off an island in 1775 which he called *La Isla de Nuestra Señora de los Angeles*, or the Island of Our Lady of the Angels. The name was anglicized on maps as Angel Island in 1826, although it was also known as Wood Island and later as Los Angeles Island. About a mile square, this island has had a busy history. In the 1850s, President Fillmore declared the island to be a military reservation. Soldiers occupied the island from 1863 until 1962. Called the "Ellis Island of the West," thousands of Oriental immigrants were processed through here from 1910 until 1940. A quarantine station also existed on this island from 1892 until 1939. It is now a state park.

BAKER'S BEACH   Named for the Baker family, whose dairy ranch was known as the Golden Gate ranch in the 1860s. This beach tucked between Lincoln Park and the Golden Gate Bridge is probably the closest thing to a Southern California style beach in San Francisco.

CANDLESTICK PARK   This stadium is on land which is adjacent to Candlestick Cove, named for a tall offshore rock which looked like a candelabra. This land form disappeared and most of the cove was filled in by the State Highway Department to make way for a freeway in 1954; however, the name of the area remained. The second oldest baseball park in the National League, it is famed for its brisk winds, weather, and struggling teams.

THE CANNERY   Originally the canning factory for the Del Monte Fruit Company, this complex of shops and restaurants now sports the Del Monte logo, a star in a circle.

CHINATOWN   Chinese settlers have lived in this part of the city since its beginning. Driven from Kwangtung province in southern China by civil war and famine, the Chinese arrived by the thousands in the 1850s. Many worked in the gold country while others came to work on the Central Pacific (later the Southern Pacific) Railroad. They were called "Crocker's Pets," because Charles Crocker—one of the Big Four—masterminded their immigration. These immigrants were subjected to intense racial harrassment during the depression of the "Terrible 70s."

Most settled in Chinatown, some opening restaurants and laundries. For years, these new Americans were the manual labor pool in this city.

COIT TOWER Named for Lillie Hitchcock Coit who left funds to beautify the city in 1929. She wanted to create a memorial to the volunteer firemen. As a young girl, Lillie was a mascot of a fire engine house, Knickerbocker Company Number 5. As she grew older, she became one of the city's grandest eccentrics, given to chasing fire engines and visiting the Barbary Coast in male garb. Above the entrance to the tower is a relief plaque of the Phoenix, the mythical bird reborn in fire, which is also the symbol of San Francisco appearing on the city's flag and seal. Contrary to public opinion, however, the Phoenix does not symbolize San Francisco's rebirth after the Fire of 1906, but instead commemorates the many deadly fires of the Gold Rush years.

CONTRA COSTA COUNTY An appropriate name for the land on the other side of the Bay from the Presidio and Mission Dolores. It was so named by the Spanish explorers and means "the opposite coast."

COW HOLLOW Named for the cows that pastured in this area, once watered by the little creeks from the surrounding hills. It boasted a respectable natural growth of grass, which improved the more it was pastured. Early San Francisco's milk came from Cow Hollow. Indeed, during the 1860s, George Hatman began a dairy ranch on several acres in this area; by the 1880s, the Board of Health ordered all the cattle in the city to be moved to less populous areas.

DALY CITY John Daly subdivided his dairy farm after the earthquake and fire of 1906. It was located south of San Francisco on the present site of this community.

FARALLON ISLANDS This word in Spanish means "cliff." This is exactly what these seven islands are. Even though they are 32 miles out in the Pacific Ocean, they are a part of the City and County of San Francisco. They are now inhabited only by birds. They were originally called Islands of Saint James by Drake (1579); the Sebastian Vizcaíno expedition (1602–03) renamed them "the Friars." Juan Francisco de Bodega y Quadra, another Spanish explorer, called these islands Farallones de los Frayles, or "cliffs or small pointed islands in the sea of the friars," in 1775. The present name is an Americanized contraction of Bodega's appellation. During the Gold Rush, eggs from the Farallon Islands sold for one dollar each in San Francisco.

FISHERMAN'S WHARF This is the home of San Francisco's commercial fishing fleet, where the fishermen return with their daily catch, often including anchovies, striped bass, sole, sand dabs, and, of course, crabs. As a tourist attraction, this area is the second most popular place in California, being surpassed only by Disneyland.

FORT FUNSTON Named in honor of Major General Frederick Funston (1865–1917), a hero of the Spanish-American War who was in command of the Department of California at the time of the earthquake and fire in 1906. It is situated along the Pacific Coast in the southwestern portion of the city.

FORT MASON   In 1882, this military reservation was named for Colonel Richard B. Mason, a military governor of California after the American occupation and during the gold discovery. His reports confirmed the discovery and set off the Gold Rush. Fort Mason is now, in part, a cultural center, housing scores of art galleries, museums, theatres, and offices for kindred groups.

FORT MILEY   Named in honor of Lieutenant Colonel John D. Miley who died in Manila on September 19, 1899, during the Spanish-American War.

FORT POINT   This name was applied by the Coast Survey in 1851 because of ruins of an old Spanish fort, the Castillo de San Joaquin. When Captain Ayala sailed into the Bay in 1775, he named it Punta de San José. The present fort was built between 1853 and 1861 on the site of the original Presidio to protect the approaches to the city. In 1882, its name was changed to Fort Winfield Scott after a former Commander-in-Chief of the Army. The run—or walk—from the Embarcadero to Fort Point is one of the most magnificent in the world.

GHIRARDELLI SQUARE   In 1897, Domingo Ghirardelli moved his chocolate and spice factory to this location on North Point Street, taking over the brick buildings abandoned by the Columbia Woolen Mills. The factory complex was transformed into the present array of shops and restaurants by William Matson Roth in the late 1960s.

GOLDEN GATE   Although the area is frequently covered by fog, pioneer explorer John Frémont was so impressed with its beauty in 1846 that he named it, in his words, "Chrysopylae or Golden Gate, for the same reason that the harbor of Byzantium was called Chrysoceras or Golden Horn." Today, it is the site of the tallest and second-longest span steel bridge in the world. It connects Marin County with San Francisco. The Golden Gate Bridge was the only major public project built in the United States without federal aid.

HUNTERS POINT   This name comes from one of two possible sources. In 1849, Robert E. Hunter and his brother, Philip Schuyler, participated in a project to develop on this point of land a city which was to be called South San Francisco. Alternatively, this area was known as Hunters Point because sportsmen went hunting there.

LAKE MERCED   Named after The Feast of Our Lady of Mercy by the Franciscan Padre Palóu when the Heceta expedition arrived on its shores on or about September 24, 1775.

MARIN COUNTY   There are two versions concerning the origin of the name. It could be after a captured Indian who became such an outstanding navigator that he was called *El Marinero,* or "the Sailor". The name was originally applied to Marin Island by an Indian who lived on it. Since the bay on which this island lies was called *Bahía de la Marinera* in 1775, the name may actually have been derived from this earlier name. See also Marin Street.

MISSION DOLORES   This mission is actually named Mission San Francisco de Asís and was dedicated on October 9, 1776, by Friar Francisco

Palóu. The mission is one of 21 established by the Franciscans along the California coast from San Diego—where the first was erected by Padre Junípero Serra on July 16, 1769—to Sonoma, which was constructed in 1823. The San Francisco mission acquired its popular name from the Laguna de Nuestra Señora de Los Dolores, a nearby body of water named after the Virgin of Sorrows because the Spanish explorers discovered it on her feast day. Excluding the adobe brick structure – of which only a few bricks remain – at the Officers Club in the Presidio, Mission Dolores is the oldest building in San Francisco. The cemetery here is a delightful spot.

MOUNT DAVIDSON Named for George Davidson, a government surveyor, who surveyed the peak in 1852 and called it Blue Mountain. It was renamed in 1911, and at 938 feet is the highest point in the city. It is the site of the annual sunrise Easter services under a 103–foot concrete cross.

MOUNT DIABLO This is the Spanish word for "devil" and it was so named by the Spanish explorers after an Indian Medicine Man they encountered in a skirmish who looked like the devil himself in his battle garb.

MOUNT OLYMPUS One story indicates that this hill was named for "Old Limpus" Hanrahan, a crippled neighborhood milk peddler. Another suggests that it was named after Mount Olympus in Greece because it had a view that was "fit for the Gods."

MOUNT TAMALPAIS The Tamales were Indians living in what is now Marin County. Their word for mountain is believed to be "pais." The name may have referred to the people living at the base of the mountain. (See also Tamalapais Terrace in the street section of this book.)

MOUNTAIN LAKE Called *Laguna de Loma Alta* or the Lake of the High Hill, referring to the 400–foot elevation of the Presidio near which this lake was observed to be situated, by Anza's party when they explored this area in 1776.

NAPA COUNTY An Indian word for either "house," "motherland," or "grizzly bear."

NOB HILL First called "Fern Hill," "the Clay Street Hill" and "the California Street Hill," there are two possible explanations for the origin of this name. The first is that "Nob" is a contraction of the word "Knob" meaning an isolated rounded hill or mountain (this would appear to be a logical name for this 338-foot high hill.) A second, and perhaps more likely, possibility is derived from the fact that wealthy San Franciscans – called "nabobs" – lived here in the 1870s and 1880s and might have given this hill its name. "Nabob" is a British slang word for wealthy person. It comes from the Hindu *Nawwah* meaning governor or vice-agent. The word was used by the English to describe the ostentatious ex-colonists who returned to Great Britain with riches acquired in India. The first residence was built on the summit on Mason Street near Sacramento Street by Dr. Arthur Hayne in 1856. Several great mansions were to be found here of which all but one were destroyed by the great fire of 1906. The one that remained was the Flood mansion built of Connecticut brownstone. It now houses the Pacific Union Club at Mason and California Streets. Diagonally across the street is the block which was the site of the Hopkins mansion (now the site of the

Mark Hopkins Hotel) and the Stanford mansion (now the site of the Stanford Court Hotel). The Crocker mansion became the site of the Grace Episcopal Cathedral at Taylor and California Streets and diagonally opposite this site is the Huntington Hotel, once the location of the Huntington mansion. Across the street sat the Colton mansion, now the site of Huntington Park. Crocker erected a two story plank fence around the establishment of an undertaker, Nicholas Young, who refused to sell his house and lot to Crocker at a price which Crocker deemed reasonable.

NORTH BEACH The name originated in the 1850s when a finger of the Bay extended far inland between Telegraph and Russian Hills, and its neighborhood was a sunny stretch of shore. It has been the historic site of San Francisco's Italian community.

PEACE PLAZA A landmark at the Japanese Cultural and Trade Center designed to symbolize the amicable relationship between the United States and Japan.

PETALUMA Means "flat back" or "flat place" in the Indian Miwok language.

PORTSMOUTH PLAZA Until 1927 this area was called Portsmouth Square. It was the center of activity for the more than thirty residents of Yerba Buena when Captain John Montgomery disembarked from his vessel, the war sloop *Portsmouth,* on July 9, 1846, and raised the United States flag. It is now the site of a small park.

POTRERO HILL The top of this hill once served as a *potrero* for the cattle of Mission Dolores. The word means "pasture" in Spanish.

PRESIDIO This is the Spanish word for "garrison" or "fortified barracks." The Presidio of San Francisco was established in 1776 and has been a military post continuously since that time. Today, it is the largest and oldest such urban military installation in the country and is a national landmark. It is the headquarters of the United States Sixth Army. If the army should ever leave, the land will automatically become part of the Golden Gate Recreational Area.

RINCON HILL Early settlers referred to the southern tip of the Yerba Buena Cove as Rincon (Spanish for "corner") Point, and the hill rising from its base as Rincon Hill. This hill is located under the approach ramp of the Bay Bridge near its San Francisco terminus. It was a true "rincon" until a part of the waterfront was filled in. From the mid 1850s until the early 1880s, this area was one of the city's most fashionable neighborhoods. In 1869, however, its demise began when Second Street, once the area's main shopping street, was cut through. Additionally, the appearance of laborers' tents nearby and the proximity to noxious industries hastened the change from a quality residential to a commercial area.

RUSSIAN HILL One undocumented story suggests that this area was named after the Russian soldiers and/or sailors who were buried near the top of this 312-foot hill in the city's early days. The children in the city in the middle of the nineteenth century, playing among the graves, began to refer to the hill as "Russian."

SAN FRANCISCO Originally called El Paraje de Yerba Buena, "the place of the good herb," the village's name was changed to San Francisco on January 30, 1847. The name was selected by Washington A. Bartlett, a Spanish-speaking lieutenant on the U.S.S. *Portsmouth* who had become the highest municipal officer in town. The name was selected to honor the Bay on which the town was situated and the nearby Mission San Francisco de Asis, better known as Mission Dolores. Although Bartlett lacked the authority, he published his proclamation in *The California Star* anyway and on January 30, 1847, the American military governor made the new name official. There is no compelling reason for the city of San Francisco to have become the great nexus of California during the Gold Rush. Oakland, or what later became Oakland, would have done just as well, as might have Benecia at the Carquinez Straits. In fact, it was word of a move by some early settlers to develop a town called Francisca (at what is now Benecia) that inspired Bartlett. (See also San Francisco Bay, below.)

SAN FRANCISCO BAY The name San Francisco came about through a geographical mix-up. In 1575, Sebastian Cermeño landed at Drake's Bay and (re)named it for the founder of the Franciscan order, St. Francis of Assisi. (Like Drake, Cermeño missed the large harbor, a few miles to the south.) When the Bay was at last discovered by the explorer Portolá in 1769, it was confused with Cermeño's (or Drake's) bay and given the bay's Spanish name. One of the world's greatest harbors, San Francisco Bay today encompasses slightly more than 400 square miles. Despite its size, it is remarkably shallow. Two thirds of it is less than 18 feet at low tide. Much of the Bay has been reclaimed, a practice which stopped in the 1970s. The Bay was originally 660 square miles but now much of San Francisco downtown, Foster City, the Berkeley waterfront, and other Bay front enclaves lie on filled land which was once the Bay itself.

SAN QUENTIN Named for a renegade Indian, Quinten, captured in the area in 1824. Ten years later, a land grant, Rancho Punta de Quintin, was named for him. The name was changed to the present spelling and the *San* added by American mapmakers, who had a tendency to "saint-ize" names in the 1850s. Now it is the name for and site of an overcrowded state prison which houses, among other inmates, Sirhan Sirhan.

SAN RAFAEL Named by the Franciscan monks for St. Rafael, the angel of body healing. The name was originally given to Mission San Rafael which was an offshoot of San Francisco's Mission Dolores. This new mission was aptly named because the monks used it as a mental hospital for Indians.

SAUSALITO Derived from the Spanish word for "sauce" or "willow," which Captain Ayala used in referring to this place in 1775 because of the willow trees growing along its streams. The correct Spanish was mentioned in 1826 and was used for the land grant to William A. Richardson in 1838. Since then, the spelling of the name has gone through many changes until the present one was used when the city was incorporated in 1893.

SONOMA COUNTY An Indian word for "nose" and it may refer either to a nose-shaped landscape feature or to a local Chief with a prominent proboscis.

TIBURON   The peninsula on which this town lies and after which it takes its name probably comes from the Spanish, *Ponte de Tiburon* or "shark's point" because of its physical resemblance to a shark nose when viewed on a map.

TELEGRAPH HILL   From early in 1849, a signal announcing the arrival of ships was located on top of this hill. In September, 1853, the first telegraph line in California, six miles in length, was completed. It connected Point Lobos at the Golden Gate with what became known as Telegraph Hill. It is one of the city's most often visited hills, even though it is one of the lower ones, standing only 295 feet high. Much of the east face of the hill has been quarried for many purposes: to be used as bulkheads, ballast to stabilize empty homeward-bound boats, or for street paving. Most of this occurred in the fifteen year period before the turn of the century.

TREASURE ISLAND   At the time it was built in the late 1930s, it was the largest man-made island in the world with 403 acres. The land was dredged from the shoals of the Bay. Situated just off Yerba Buena Island, it was the site of the 1939 Golden Gate International Exposition. It was originally intended to be an airport; it is now a naval base. There are three versions concerning the origin of the name. The silt drawn from the shoals was believed by many to contain flecks of gold from the Mother Lode. Another maintains that the name was selected "because it expressed a glamorously beautiful, almost fabulous island that would present the treasures of the world." The third explanation suggests that it was named after the book by San Francisco's beloved storyteller, Robert Louis Stevenson.

TWIN PEAKS   An Indian legend says that Twin Peaks was originally one mountain (man and wife) split into two by the Great Spirit with a bolt of lightning because the couple was so argumentative. When the Spanish came to Yerba Buena they referred to the peaks as Los Pechos de la Choca, in English "the breasts of the Indian maiden." One of San Francisco's most stunning views can be seen from atop Twin Peaks—the second and fourth tallest hills in San Francisco (910 and 904 feet).

UNION SQUARE   This park was given to the city by Mayor John Geary in 1850. Eleven years later, on May 11, a large public meeting was held in this park to decide whether or not San Francisco should secede during the Civil War. The placards in the square quoted Daniel Webster and said, "The Union, the whole Union and nothing but the Union" and "Liberty and Union, Now and Forever, One and Inseparable." The square became the recognized rallying ground of Unionists, led by Unitarian minister Thomas Starr King. In the middle of The Square, one may find a monument erected to honor Admiral George Dewey who defeated the Spanish fleet in Manila Bay during the Spanish-American War.

WALNUT CREEK   Named after the Spanish *arroyo de los Nogales* or "creek of the Walnuts."

WESTERN ADDITION   In the 1860s Larkin Street was the western boundary of the city; when an addition to it went up west of the town border, it became known as the Western Addition.

YERBA BUENA ISLAND The original name for San Francisco. It means "good herb" in Spanish. The name came from the wild mint which grew all over the sand dunes which were once to be found here.

If you have information or a favorite story that corrects or explains the origin of a street name not listed here, please write to me care of Lexikos at 4079 19th Avenue, San Francisco, CA 94132.

Louis K. Loewenstein

APPENDIX

Throughout their history, the streets of San Francisco have had their names changed frequently. In the earliest years, Pacific Avenue was called Bartlett, Sacramento named Howard, and Battery called Sloat. Patriots in World War I renamed Berlin Street, Brussels Street; during World War II, Japan Street became Colin P. Kelly Street.

Many of these changes have been mentioned in the text where I have been able to discover the origins of the current (or the past) name. But almost two hundred streets exist whose name origins are lost to history. The only record available is often the date of a name change, for instance when Treat Alley was renamed Trainor in 1909.

Below, I have listed name changes which were not mentioned in the text. Unfortunately for the researcher, the reasons for the changes were never recorded. Many were made to clear up confusion between streets, alleys, and places, but just as frequently, the motive seems to have been historical or even (as in the case of plain Mary Street transformed to illustrious Homer) whimsical.

Current Name / *Previous Name* / Date Changed   Current Name / *Previous Name* / Date Changed

Abbey Street / *Alemany Street* / 1909
Acton Street / *Henrietta Street* / 1882
Addison Street / *Lewis Street* / 1882
Adele Court / *Ade Alley* / 1928
Alert Court / *Albert Alley* / 1909
Ames Street / *Alder Alley* / 1909
Amity Alley / *Ada Alley* / 1909
Anson Place / *Ankeny Place* / 1909
Anthony Street / *New Anthony Street* / 1909
Appleton Avenue / *Hudson Street* / 1882 /
    and *West Avenue* / 1909
Ashton Avenue / *Arlington Avenue* / 1909
Banks Street / *Ward Street* / 1882
Barneveld Street / *Railroad Avenue* / 1882
Beaver Street / *Tilden Street* / 1909
Beckett Street / *Bartlett Alley* / 1909
Bennington Street / *Scott Street* / 1882
Berwick Place / *Mariposa Terrace* / 1909
Beverly Street / *Thorton Street* / 1909
Bishop Street / *Burnside Street* / 1909
Black Place / *Bay View Place* / 1909
Bolana Street / *North Avenue* / 1909
Boutwell Street / *Hampshire Street* / 1882
Boylston Street / *King Street* / 1882
Boyton Court / *Belcher Court* / 1909
Bradford Street / *Mercer Street* / 1895
Brant Alley / *Broad Alley* / 1909
Breen Place / *Browns Alley* / 1909
Brice Terrace / *Bryant Terrace* / 1909
Bromley Place / *Webster Place* / 1909

Brompton Avenue / *Fulton Avenue* / 1909
Bronte Street / *Harrison* / 1882
Brush Place / *Bruce Place* / 1909
Burke Avenue / *Second Avenue South* / 1909
Burnside Avenue / *Kingston Avenue* / 1882
Butte Place / *Brannan Place* / 1909
Byxbee Street / *Ford Street* / 1882
Campbell Avenue / *Barry Street* / 1909
Campton Place / *Stockton Place* / 1909
Central Avenue / *Lott Street* / 1895
Cherney Street / *Glenn Avenue* / 1909
Child Street / *Good Children Street* / 1909
Chilton Avenue / *Clinton Avenue* / 1909
Churchill Street / *Church Avenue* / 1909
Claude Lane / *Clara Lane* / 1909
Clifford Terrace / *Sixteenth Street* / 1909
Clyde Street / *Liberty Street* / 1882
Coleridge Street / *California Avenue* / 1909
Collingwood Street / *Sherman Street* / 1882
Columbia Square Street / *Columbia Street* /
    1882
Conkling Street / *Vermont Street* / 1882
Cordelia Street / *Virginia Place* / 1882
Corwin Street / *Stanton Street* / 1909
Cosmo Place / *Lewis Place* / 1909
Cowell Place / *Flint Alley* / 1909
Crystal Street / *Milton Street* / 1882
Cumberland Street / *Columbia Street* / 1882
Cunningham Place / *Cumberland Place* //1909
Cushman Street / *Yerba Buena Street* / 1909

105

Cyrus Place / *Morse Place* / 1909
Daggett Street / *South Street* / 1909
Danvers Street / *Rose Street* / 1882
Darrell Place / *Norton Avenue* / 1909
Delano Avenue / *Delaware Avenue* / 1909
De Long Street / *Schiller Street* / 1882
Deming Street / *Eighteenth Street* / 1909
Derby Street / *Oak Street* / 1882
Drummond Street / *Eureka Alley* / 1909
Eastman Street / *West End Alley* / 1909
Edgardo Street / *Edgar Street* / 1909
Ellington Avenue / *Porter Avenue* / 1909
Emerson Street / *Obsidiana Lane* / 1970
Ewing Place / *Metcalf Place* / 1882
Fargo Place / *Columbia Place* / 1882
Fielding Street / *Newell Street* / 1882
Fitzgerald Avenue / *Thirtieth Avenue South* / 1909
Flournoy Street / *Prim Street* / 1924
Garfield Street / *Sherman Street* / 1882
Gorham Street / *Garden Lane* / 1912
Granville Way / *Grafton Street* / 1919
Grote Place / *Grant Place* / 1909
Grover Place / *Gavin Place* / 1909
Hallam Street / *Harrison Avenue* / 1909
Hamerton Avenue / *Hamilton Avenue* / 1909
Harlow Street / *Hardy Street* / 1909
Harper Street / *Bartlett Street* / 1882
Hastings Terrace / *Lincoln Place* / 1909
Havelock Street / *Henry Street* / 1882
Head Street / *Florence Street* / 1882
Highland Avenue / *East Avenue* / 1909
Hilton Street / *Lee Street* / 1909
Holladay Street / *Heath Street* / 1909
Homer Street / *Mary Street* / 1882
Ils Lane / *Maiden Lane* / 1922
James Alley / *Jackson Alley* / 1909
Jarobe Avenue / *Jefferson Avenue* / 1909
Jasper Place / *Union Place* / 1909
Jerrold Avenue / *Tenth Avenue South* / 1909
Judson Avenue / *Wieland Avenue* / 1899
Keith Street / *K Street South* / 1909
Lamartine Street / *Cotta Street* / 1909
Lansing Street / *Laurel Place* / 1909
Lawrence Avenue / *Sherman Avenue* / 1909
Ledyard Street / *Emma Street* / 1882
Leona Terrace / *Lyon Terrace* / 1909
Levant Street / *Juno Street* / 1914
Linda Street / *Angelica Street* / 1945
Lippard Avenue / *Park Avenue* / 1882
Locksley Avenue / *Serpentine Road* / 1909
Lowell Street / *Humboldt Street* / 1882
Lucky Street / *Garfield Avenue* / 1909
Lusk Street / *Crooks Street* / 1961
Marcy Place / *Vernon Place* / 1882
Margrave Place / *Margaret Place* / 1909

Marston Avenue / *Milton Avenue* / 1909
Maynard Street / *Marshall Street* / 1909
Merlin Street / *Madison Street* / 1909
Miguel Street / *San Miguel Street* / 1938
Miller Place / *Miles Place* / 1909
Montague Place / *Moulton Place* / 1909
Murray Street / *South Avenue* / 1909
Newburg Street / *New Grove Avenue* / 1909
Niantic Avenue / *East Railroad Avenue* / 191
Nordhoff Street / *Midway Street* / 1909
Oakdale Avenue / *Fifteenth Avenue South* / 1909
Ogden Avenue / *Old Hickory Street* / 1909
Ordway Street / *Irving Street* / 1882
Osgood Place / *Ohio Avenue* / 1909
Otsego Avenue / *West Lake Avenue* / 1909
Parkhurst Alley / *Parker Alley* / 1909
Parsons Street / *Parkside Avenue* / 1909
Paulding Street / *Paul Street* / 1909
Payson Street / *Park Way* / 1909
Peabody Street / *Byrne Street* / 1882
Pelton Place / *Pacific Alley* / 1909
Powers Avenue / *Powell Avenue* / 1909
Pratt Place / *Ellick Lane* / 1913
Prescott Court / *Ohio Avenue* / 1882
Quane Street / *Quince Alley* / 1909
Ramsell Street / *State Street* / 1882
Randall Street / *Palmer Street* / 1909
Ridgewood Avenue / *Hamburg Street* / 1927
Ripley Street / *Prospect Place* / 1882
Rockdale Drive / *San Martin Avenue* / 1939
Rockland Street / *Brady Place* / 1882
Rodgers Street / *Folsom Alley* / 1909
Romolo Place / *Pinkey Place* / 1913
Roscoe Street / *Decatur Street* / 1882
Rosemont Place / *Maple Court* / 1909
Rowland Street / *St. Charles Street* / 1882
Rutland Street / *Allen Street* / 1882
Sabin Place / *Salina Place* / 1909
Santa Rosa Avenue / *Croke Street* / 1911
Sargent Street / *Central Street* / 1882
Sawyer Street / *Fay Street* / 1909
Severn Street / *Medway Alley* / 1909
Shannon Street / *William Street* / 1909
Sloan Alley / *Tehama Alley* / 1909
Southard Place / *Randall Place* / 1909
Spring Street / *Webb Street* / 1909
Staples Avenue / *Spreckels Avenue* / 1909
Stark Street / *Polk Street* / 1882
Stillman Street / *Silver Street* / 1909
Taber Place / *Park Lane North* / 1909
Tenny Place / *Tehama Place* / 1909
Thomas Avenue / *Twentieth Avenue* / 1909
Thrift Street / *Hill Street* / 1882
Tomkins Avenue / *Union Avenue* / 1909
Tracy Place / *Vallejo Alley* / 1909

Trainor Street / *Treat Alley* / 1909
Treasury Place / *Burnett Place* / 1909
Trumbull Street / *Lewis Street* / 1882
Valmar Terrace / *Moscow Street* / 1955
Varennes Street / *Lafayette Place* / 1909
Varney Place / *Park Lane South* / 1909
Verdi Place / *Montgomery Court* / 1909
Vinton Court / *Virginia Court* / 1909
Wall Place / *Coolidge Place* / 1912
Warner Place / *Vernon Place* / 1909
Washburn Street / *Washington Avenue* / 1909

Waterville Street / *Nebraska Avenue* / 1882
Wayne Place / *Scott Place* / 1909
Wentworth Street / *Washington Place* / 1909
Wetmore Street / *Tay Street* / 1923
Whitney Street / *Palmer Street* / 1909
Wiese Street / *Linda Place* / 1916
Willard Street / *Belmont Avenue* / 1909
Willard Street North / *Willard Street* / 1882
Wilmont Street / *Widley Avenue* / 1909
Wilson Street / *Bismarck Street* / 1924
Winthrop Street / *Webster Street* / 1882
Woodland Avenue / *Lotta Street* / 1909

n 1882, the following streets and alleys were given names. The reasons why these particular names were selected are, however, lost.

Acorn Alley
Ada Court
Alder Alley (now Street)
Clarion Alley
Eaton Alley (now Place)
Edgar Place
Fisher Alley
Golden Court
Harlem Alley
Hobart Alley

Jerome Alley
Malden Alley
Mersey Alley (now Street)
Opal Place
Ophir Alley
Orange Alley
Oscar Alley
Pardee Alley
Pink Alley

Piper Loop
Redfield Alley
Shaw Alley
Spencer Alley (now Street)
Tehama Alley
Troy Alley
Tulip Alley
Wagner Alley
Waldo Alley

PACIFIC AVENUE AT PRESIDIO WALL

BOOKS

Alotta, Robert. *Street Names of Philadelphia.* Philadelphia: Temple University Press, 1975.

Bakalinski, Ada. *Stairway Walks in San Francisco.* San Francisco: Lexikos, 1984.

Block, Eugene B. *The Immortal San Franciscans.* San Francisco: Chronicle Books, 1971.

Boatner, Martin M. *The Civil War Dictionary.* New York: David McKay Co. Inc., 1959.

Brown, Marion. *San Francisco Old and New.* San Francisco: The Grabhorn Press, 1939.

Carlisle, Henry C. *San Francisco Street Names.* San Francisco: American Trust Co., 1954.

Cassady, Stephen. *Spanning the Gate.* Mill Valley, Calif.: Square Books, 1979.

Cole, Tom *A Short History of San Francisco.* San Francisco: Lexikos, 1981.

Conrad, Barnaby. *San Francisco: A Profile with Pictures.* New York: Viking Press Inc., 1959.

Delehanty, Randolph. *San Francisco.* New York: The Dial Press, 1980.

Doss, Margaret Patterson. *San Francisco at Your Feet.* New York: Grove Press, 1964.

Eldredge Zoeth S. *The Beginnings of San Francisco,* Volume II. New York: John Rankin, Co., 1912.

Encyclopedia Britannica. Chicago: Fifteenth Edition, 1974.

Gudde, Erwin G. *California Place Names.* Berkeley, Calif.: University of California Press, 1949.

Hanna, Phil Townsend. *The Dictionary of California Lane Names.* Los Angeles: The Automobile Club of Southern California, 1951.

Hansen, Gladys. *The San Francisco Almanac.* San Francisco: Chronicle Books, 1978.
           The San Francisco Almanac. Novato: Presidio Press, 1980.

Harder, Kelsie B., editor. *Illustrated Dictionary of Place Names: United States and Canada.* New York: Facts on File Publications, 1985.

Hart, James. *A Companion to California.* New York: Oxford University Press, 1978.

Larousse Encyclopedia of Mythology. New York: Prometheus Press, 1959.

Levinson, John. *Cow Hollow.* San Francisco: San Francisco Yesterday, 1976.

Lockwood, Charles. *Suddenly San Francisco.* San Francisco: California Living Book, 1978.

Lotchin, Rodger W. *San Francisco 1846-1856: From Hamlet to City.* New York: Oxford University Press, 1974.

McCarthy, Rev. Frances T. *Hunters Point.* San Francisco: Flores Paramount Press, 1942.

McDowell, Jack, editor. *San Francisco.* Menlo Park, Calif.: Lane Magazine and Book Company, 1969.

McGloin, John B. *San Francisco, The Story of a City.* San Rafael, Calif.: Presidio Press, 1978.

Moscow, Henry. *The Street Book.* New York: Hagstrom Company Inc., 1978.

Myrick, David F. *San Francisco's Telegraph Hill.* Berkeley, Calif.: Howell-North Books, 1972.

Reps, John W. *Cities of the American West.* Princeton, N.J.: Princeton University Press.

Rowland, Leon. *Los Fundadores.* Fresno: Academy of California Church History, 1951.

Soule, Frank, Gihon, John, and Nisbett, James. *The Annals of San Francisco.* Palo Alto, Calif.: Lewis Osborne, 1966.

REPORTS AND OTHER DOCUMENTS

Adams, Elizabeth G. *Street Names in San Francisco.* An unpublished paper, 1954.

A Guide to Historic San Francisco. San Francisco History Room, San Francisco Public Library 1980.

Colorful Place Names of Northern California. Wells Fargo Bank, San Francisco: 1974.

Municipal Record of San Francisco, 1882 and 1909.

Murphy, Edward. *The Thoroughfares of San Francisco.* An unpublished and undated paper.

Official Journal of the Proceedings of the Board of Supervisors, Volume IV, November, 1909

San Francisco Directory, 1861.

MAGAZINE ARTICLES

Brown, Thomas P. "San Francisco's Century-Old Street Names—The Happy Valley Day of '49," *The Time Card*, San Francisco: The Transportation Club of San Francisco March, 1949.

Maupin, Armistead. "The Streets of San Francisco," *New West*, Los Angeles: May 2 1977.

San Jose Pioneer Magazine, September 15, 1897.

Wheelan, Albert P. "The Streets, Avenues, Alleys and Lanes of South of Market—Th Story of Their Origin," *South of Market Journal*, San Francisco: April, 1927.

NEWSPAPERS

Fitzhammon, E. G. "The Streets of San Francisco," *San Francisco Chronicle,* August 27, 1928 March 31, 1929.

San Francisco Chronicle, various issues.

San Francisco Examiner, various issues.

Tukman, John. "Naming History," *Mt. Tamalpais Blazer,* January 24, 1985.